Change the World—Write Your Song!

Change the World—Write Your Song!

Fundamentals and Beyond for the Aspiring Singer/Songwriter - Book I

Jena Douglas

www.jenadouglas.com

iUniverse, Inc.
Bloomington

Change the World—Write Your Song!
Fundamentals and Beyond for the Aspiring Singer/Songwriter - Book I

iUniverse books may be ordered through booksellers or by contacting:

iUniverse
1663 Liberty Drive
Bloomington, IN 47403
www.iuniverse.com
1-800-Authors (1-800-288-4677)

Because of the dynamic nature of the Internet, any web addresses or links contained in this book may have changed since publication and may no longer be valid. The views expressed in this work are solely those of the author and do not necessarily reflect the views of the publisher, and the publisher hereby disclaims any responsibility for them.

Any people depicted in stock imagery provided by Thinkstock are models, and such images are being used for illustrative purposes only.
Certain stock imagery © Thinkstock.

ISBN: 978-1-4620-3812-1 (sc)
ISBN: 978-1-4620-3813-8 (hc)
ISBN: 978-1-4620-3814-5 (ebk)

Library of Congress Control Number: 2011916987

Printed in the United States of America

iUniverse rev. date: 11/10/2011

For my son Dylan

TABLE OF CONTENTS

Foreword by Apryl Hill

If you've stopped to look at this book, there's a song in you trying to get out! You're looking for that something to inspire you, tell you how to bring out what's inside of you. You have something to say! And what better way than in a song! And as you've probably noticed, there are a "Kabillion" music books out there. Why this one? I've been a songwriter/musician all my life and most books I've picked up made my eyes gloss over and I felt defeated. Quite simply, Jena's written a book of education, inspiration and experience, straight to the heart of songwriting.

Songs have been the voice of every generation and some songs are immortal. You can tell the era and what was happening in the world and how people were feeling at that time in history. How and what people were feeling and experiencing at that moment in time was captured in a song. Music and song is very powerful! How many times have you heard or said, "That's my song!"

I've known Jena Douglas a good part of my life. We met thru music and played in a band together. We became a local "Hit Band" in Santa Barbara, California. Really the first time we ever heard one of our songs playing on the local radio station occurred while we were walking down Main Street. We recognized our song playing on the radio of a convertible car stopped at a red light. We scared that poor person, running over to their car screaming, "That's our song!" "That's us!" "That's us!" It was a surreal and unforgettable moment to this day.

Jena went on to formally study music and received a B. A. degree. She's an active member of numerous song camps, house concerts and more that you will discover. It's an incredibly supportive community. With Jena's lifelong vast experience and education, and knowing the challenges we've all faced, Jena went about to produce this book, this work of art to help others "Write your song" "Change The World!"

Apryl Hill
Musician/Songwriter

Preface

The idea for this book was conceived over a Greek cup of coffee and an enlightening conversation with my friends, Steve and Mariella Stockmal. Steve and Mariella know how to make you feel welcomed! They own a music school in Goleta, CA called "Studio Music Group," and they have a set of books on various music topics. They encouraged me to write my own book. They said it was easy. While I have all the qualifications for writing on this subject it has been far from easy. I was intimidated by the massive amount of work it was going to take, but Steve and Mariella shared a secret with me. It was the movie, _The Secret._ Suddenly, a light went on in the attic of this fuzz ball brain of mine. Everything I have ever done up to this point came together! It was an epiphany! For you see, I love to write (I'm a songwriter) and I have a real passion for sharing the benefits of songwriting! And . . . I can write a book!

I have enjoyed every moment putting this book together. I loved going through my old school notes and books. It felt good to reacquaint myself with music theory and history, but it took me a long time to finish this book. I started it in 2008, but quickly got discouraged by seeing all the books out on songwriting already. Then I lost my job, moved out of town and was again inspired to finish the book to generate an income. After attending some marketing seminars online (webinars) for new authors, I realized, "What this world needs are more soul searchin', idealistic, Utopian songwriters!" We need songwriters who speak with their hearts to get the conversations going. And from the depths of a songwriter's soul comes a world of honest communication and respect. OK, it's a lot to ask for but I was on fire! The book became more than just a how-to book, but a worldly self-help book too! And that's what finished this book. I got my Mojo back!

It's funny but I feel like I am over-qualified to write this book because I've been using songwriting as a self-help tool for years! I know a lot about music but from personal experience, I know more about the benefits of songwriting as therapy! I have always written songs that are personal in nature. When I was feeling sad, hurt or angry, I would write a song as a way to bring whatever I was feeling to the surface, but after seeing "The Secret" and learning about the "law of attraction," I found that the energy I spent on writing about negative feelings was coming back to haunt me. The law of attraction is, "like attracts like" (quantum physics)[1]. So, if I am writing songs about sadness, hurt and anger then I am attracting more sadness, hurt and anger into my life. And I don't know about you but I don't need it! Once more the light went off in my head! But wait! What about the passion and the dynamics that conflict bring to music? You have to be able to express "a full spectrum of emotions" to keep a listener (and a songwriter) interested. For me, feeling the dynamics of each opposing emotion is the reason I write! It's the raw emotions that appeal to me. After all, this world would suck if all we had were cutesy little monotonic happy songs (think: It's A Small World After All).

I love all types of music, even monotonic happy songs, when I'm in the mood, (except: It's A Small World After All) but there's something I don't understand. Do I need to be a cookie cutter writer of Utopian ideals to truly be happy? No! It's my world and I create it, the way I want it! At any rate, how am I to know what I am feeling sometimes unless I explore those feelings? In the book, *Excuse Me, Your Life Is Waiting-the astonishing power if feelings* by Lynn Grabhorn she talks about the law of attraction and how she uses it in her life. For example, "Hooray for Negative . . . Every negative emotion we've ever had, no matter how meek or well hidden has come from the lack of what we really wanted."[2] Basically she is saying, negative emotions will help you find what it is that you want by telling you what it is you don't want. Aha! I've been doing that all along but I need to also include the happy moments and feelings into my songwriting. So, when I play those happy songs I'll bring more happiness into my life! Duh! But to be fair, I don't think that if you only write and perform sad songs you'll never get any happiness. I just think you'll get a lot more happiness because you'll be attracting more happiness! The power of writing and performing a song is like having the power to heal yourself.

---

[1]   Byrne, *The Secret*, 7.

[2]   Grabhorn, *Excuse Me Your Life Is Waiting*, 69.

I am a single mother of a very talented singer/songwriter who has Asperger's Syndrome (autism). He is very high functioning. What I mean by high functioning is, unless you are familiar with signs of autism, you would not know that he is autistic. In an Internet article by Dr. Staum, she states, "Music Therapy is the unique application of music to enhance personal lives by creating positive changes in human behavior." She continues, "Music therapists traditionally work with autistic children because of this unusual responsiveness which is adaptable to non-music goals." [3] She talks a lot about severe cases of autism but what is important to know is that music is used by the professionals to reach someone who has a hard time communicating, especially in social settings. I see the benefits of music therapy every day with my son. He is a blend of all the songwriters he ever heard. By emulating his idols and their music he has the admiration of his peers. He is an artist after all and artists have the freedom to be a little eccentric (in fact it's assumed)! Music is a perfect fit for my highly functional autistic son. If songwriting can help him and me then songwriting can help anyone. If you're looking to make a difference in your or someone else's life, get this book. This book will not only teach you the "how-to" in songwriting but also teach you my own, soul-searchin', life changin', story tellin', songwritin' therapy tips, too!

If you write only one song in your life, I hope that it is the right song! Use this book to help you find the song you want to share with the world! This is what excites me! Imagine, songwriters as visionaries for world peace, focusing their "attention and energy to trust, love, abundance, education, and peace." [4] According to *The Secret* and other "law of attraction" believers, the world is yours to create! So, Change The World—Write Your Song! Why not? But first, let's start with you! How do you rise above the negative emotions of the times? I say, write a song! Write your song!

---

[3] Staum, Education: Music Therapy and Language. http://www.autism. com/edu_music_therapy.asp

[4] Byrne, *The Secret*, 153.

Acknowledgments

Thank you Steve and Mariella Stockmal for getting me started on this book and of course your inspiration. Thank you, my former professors and teachers at UCSB and SBCC, especially Alejandro Planchart, (UCSB) and Dr. John Clark (SBCC) and thanks to my friends, Tony Ybarra, and Ken Ryals, for many happy hours of music and mayhem. Thank you, my former guitar teacher, Michael Frey for teaching me The Who's "I'm One". Thank you Paul Zollo for being an inspiration and a friend. Thank you Gina Milone, Joyce Douglas, Darlene Douglas and Mariella Stockmal for editing. Thank you Celeste Taylor Bryant for your marketing advice. Thank you Cinder Jean for having Dylan and I open for you at Cold Spring Tavern and introducing me to Kenny Edwards. Penny Nichols and Kenny Edwards for your love and support and for invitation to the Summersongs' Family, Severin Browne, Wendy Waldman, Rosemary Butler, Renee Bodie, Jaynee Thorne, Dale La Duke, Janice Bina-Smith, Jackie Morris, Britta Lee Shain, Vince Chafin, David Roth, Sherie Davis, Randall Lamb, Penelope Salinger, Susan Marie Reeves, Mark Alciati, Sonnie Brown, Teresa McNeil MacLean, Bill Gessner, Florence Mercurio Riggs, Joyce Woodson, Rebecca Troon, Caroline Aiken, Sloan Wainwright, Dan Navarro, Teresa Tudury, Nicola Gordon, Harold Payne, Jill Knight, Arturo Tello, Barbara Coventry, Rich Phillips, Sabine Blanchard, Deborah Gromack, Don Halsell, Greg Troll, Leslie Beauvals, Joe Cicero, Renee Dickson, Jill Freeman, Elizabeth Johnson, Jeffery Beach, Jackie Arsenault, Stan DeWitt, Peggy Flinn Glenn, and especially Tara Covington and her husband Jim for all the car-pooling we did (in their car!). And thanks to the Summersongs extended family, Dana Charnofsky, Russ and Julie Paris, Freebo F. Freebo for your friendship. Thank you to former band members and players, Andy Webb, Jim Rankin, Barry Birmingham, Pete Sharpe, Todd Grant, Steve Emanuel, John Caprara, Rick Reeves, Steve Stockmal, Dylan Douglas, Aaron Douglas, Keith Douglas, Barbara Coventry, Marc Johnson, Matt Estes, and Hector Hurtado. Grace Feldman, and Robinson Eikenberry for your love of my music and friendship. Thank you, Nancy

Singelman, Kathy Kennedy, Jim and Patti Daly for your valued friendship. Thank you friends and fans that have supported me throughout my musical endeavors. Thank you, Apryl Hill and Gina Milone, for letting Dylan and me move in to your wonderful home while I finish this book. Thank you, Apryl Hill for being my friend for so long and for writing the foreword. Thank you Janine and Clark Smith for your support and love. Thanks to Aaron, Darlene, Keith and Kelly Douglas for your support and love when I needed it the most. And thanks to the rest of my family for your unending support and love. And a most important thank you to Dylan and Jake, my son and dog, who are my best friends, who lift me up when I'm down, who make me want to do and be my best. Finally, thank you Mom for unknowingly initiating the beginning of my songwriting therapy. And thank you Dad for being the biggest music fan I have ever encountered!

Introduction—I Am Who I Am.

I was born and raised in Santa Barbara, California. I am Scottish, English, Irish, Polish, German, Dutch and Native American. In short, I'm an American Mutt. And it is a part of who I am, but only a part. The predominantly English culture I live by who, loves tea w/cream and sugar and listens to "old British country rock," also lives by another culture, Spanish. Santa Barbara is a city that embraces its Spanish Heritage. And so a lot of my music is a mixture of all that! You let me know what you think? http://www.reverbnation.com/jenadouglas I've been told by music critics (hate that name) that my music is: Alt. Pop/Country. I kind of like that title, but I don't like to think about fitting into any genre. "I am who I am" and my music is about as mixed up as my blood. And when playing a song in public, the song will be influenced by mood, feelings and environment and so the genre changes. Speaking of environment, I know what you're thinking; Santa Barbara is pretty nice. I am lucky. I live in a nice environment but everyone has his or her own demons to fight and it doesn't matter where you live. After all, we are our own worst enemy! And I fought with myself for almost fifty years. I'm fifty-three now and I'm very grateful to be living in Vista, California, at the home of my friend, Apryl Hill her girlfriend, Gina Milone, my son, Dylan, my dog Jake and a slew of pets too many to count. Woof!

I wrote my first song when I was around nine or ten years old and wrote a couple of songs in high school, while enduring the teenage blues. Ugh! My mom told me that if I couldn't talk to her about what I was feeling, then I needed to "write it out on a piece of paper and burn it," but instead I wrote a song! That was my first experience of writing songs for therapy. Songwriting helped me define what I was feeling; so then I was able to resolve that feeling. It didn't always work because I didn't know anything about the "law of attraction," but it allowed me to pinpoint my emotions. Ever since then I have been using songwriting as a tool to cope with things and have learned that I am not alone. A lot of famous songwriters write songs as a way to express very deep emotions. I mean, as a teenager I listened to things like John Lennon's "Isolation" and as an adult I wrote "Random Thoughts," using a variation of words from John Lennon's song but not the melody. Songs and music, in general, are good for seizing the moment.

I grew up with the music of the late sixties and seventies. I also grew up to the Utopian ideals during that era with songs like, "All You Need Is Love" and "What The World Needs Now Is Love." The music all seemed to be pertaining to a feeling of love and peace (Yep, I'm a hippie at heart!). All through high school I loved to sing and write lyrics, but never thought about songwriting as a career until 1982 when I saw a performance of The Who that blew me away. Wow! I was so moved by the music, the words, and the dynamics of the music that I sang with my voice in "full power mode." I was not alone. I was chanting, "See Me, Feel Me, Touch Me, Heal Me!" with about sixty thousand other people. It was a Utopia of emotions that grabbed me and I thought to myself, "I want to write songs like this!" Pete Townshend's powerfully emotional style of songwriting inspired me to want to become a musician and songwriter. I was hooked and I have never looked back!

The Who inspired me to *want* to write but I am also influenced by all the songs I've ever heard! It's taken many years to consolidate "that library of songs" in my head. *Then,* I had to somehow mix "that library of songs" into my *own* songs. I knew this was going to take time. I have become the songwriter of all my favorite songwriters at once! I'm just a little bit of this song and a little piece of that song. Mix a little flamenco guitar or trumpet into the mix and, viola! My music! In songwriting you always put a little of your story into every song. You bring in environment and influences. That is what's so wonderful about songwriting.

In this book, I have compiled more than twenty-five years of music knowledge; tips on writing hit songs, the music business, but most importantly, the benefits of songwriting as therapy. I have two degrees in music; an associate of art degree and a bachelor of art degree. Having a degree in music doesn't make me the music "Maestro," it just means that I can analyze music from the past and compare it to your music when you need direction. To be fair, you don't have to know how to read music to write a song. There are plenty of prolific songwriters who don't read a note, like Diane Warren who;

"was the first songwriter in the history of Billboard to have seven hits, by different artists, on the singles chart simultaneously . . . Ms. Warren doesn't read music and snoozed through the one music theory class she ever took. She considers her lack of formal musical training to be a source of freedom. "I'm always doing things you're not supposed to do musically, but, hey, I don't know any better!"[5]

Many will tell you that The Beatles couldn't read, but they did have George Martin who was musically trained helping with their arrangements. He even played on some of their tunes (harpsichord sounding instrument on "In My Life")[6]. The magical thing about music is there are no rules. But for many others and me it helps to have a little knowledge. The most important thing in songwriting is to love doing it. Skip the section on music theory if you're not interested, but I strongly recommend that you learn an instrument. Guitar and piano are easy to learn, and in this book you will learn to play an instrument for the purpose of writing a song.

I might as well tell you right now that there are going to be areas in the songwriting process that I cannot teach you. You, as a songwriter, are everything you've ever heard and chances are you will differ from me. Each song will be your own story and your own interpretation of the feeling you want to convey in that story. You will have your own Muse (inspiration) to listen to. However, as a songwriter, it's important to know that all songs have certain things in common. I want to share them with you. I also want to continue teaching you everything involved in being a singer/songwriter, and that will take at *least* two books.

I have begun working on the second book but it is important that you embrace this first book and then pass the knowledge along. Buy this book for someone and I will give you a "Change The World; Write Your Song," T-shirt! My mission is to get everyone writing songs for therapy and for the world. Let's all write one long song around the world; that will heal and change the world for the better! I'm thinkin', peace and love are never out of fashion. There will be no peace without; if we don't have it within.

---

[5]   Toni Bently A Chart Topping Cave Dweller interview of Diane Warren (The Wall Street Journal - Oct.16,2010)

[6]   http://www.songfacts.com/detail.php?id=95

So, GET IT OUT! Embrace your inner self, be honest and true and then pass it along. GIVE IT AWAY!

You see, songwriting is more than just plucking a guitar and singing a tune. It's been a method of communication for thousands of years![7] If it hadn't been for songwriting, I know I'd probably be in a mental institution or dead. Songwriting as therapy is about opening your heart and soul into something that's bigger than you. So, "Change The World-Write Your Song!" And then while you're still incubating your ideas for saving the world, check out the second book, "Change The World-Write Your Song! Book II."

In the first book, we will discover what type of music you write naturally. We will find your style, your strengths and later learn how to categorize your music into a genre (for marketing purposes). You will learn to create original lyrics and basic chords to go with those lyrics. It is important to feel comfortable with what you know, before diving into something you don't know, like writing scores for film, etc. (Writing for film and other venues will be introduced in the second book.) You will also learn the business side to being a songwriter.

The second book will have more theory and musicianship (including vocal techniques). You will have the opportunity to write compositions for orchestration and songs for Film and TV. The second book will also help you find the right musicians for performance and recording. "Change The World-Write Your Song! Book II," will give you do's and don'ts for the Internet, studio and performance. On my own I have spent many, many hours recording, performing and promoting. But my love, my reason for being, is to write music.

So let's get started! You will need a notebook to use with this book. You can do all of the exercises in sequence or jump around. Take what you need and leave the rest. Keep in mind that comments from songwriters in this book talk about what makes a "hit song" and how to emulate those "hit songs." We don't have to agree on what makes a great song or even what makes a great song a "hit song." What we need to agree on is to accept each voice we hear, or song we sing, as a part of a whole. I am who I am as you are who you are. We are in it together. So, let your Muse free!

---

[7]   Morgan, *Mutant Message Down Under*, 110.

Thank you for choosing this songwriting book out of all the other books. I wish you many happy hours, minutes, and seconds as a songwriter, but most of all I hope you write the song you want the world to hear!

With Peace and Love,
Jena Douglas

"I pay no attention whatever to anybody's praise or blame. I simply follow my own feelings".

—Mozart

"Just as the musician seeks musical expression, so the music in the universe seeks to be expressed."

—Marlo Morgan (Aboriginal expression)[8]

"To inspire and to heal through songwriting, creating a world of peace"

—Jena Douglas.

---

[8] Morgan, *Mutant Message Down Under*, 110.

What do you want?—"We want the world and we want it . . . now!"

What makes a person go from writing songs about themselves to writing world-class songs? You have to know what you want and then ask for it. Jim Morrison of the band, The Doors, sang in his song, "When The Music's Over," the words, "We want the world and we want it . . . now!" Regardless of whom he was talking about, making that statement attracted the world to them (The Doors). What do you want out of songwriting? Whatever you want to do with your songwriting is OK because everyone has a song and should write it! For every song you write you are refining your feelings, which will help you in whatever your life's quest is. But even as you may just want to write songs as a hobby, you could make some money, too.

What this book can do for you is to help you discover your song or your voice. There is a purpose for you to write your song and distribute it out into the airwaves regardless of what magnitude the waveform is. If you sing it to yourself or share it with the world this book will help you discover your inner songwriter. Through music you will discover that you are the master of your universe (so be easy on yourself). According to the "law of attraction," what you are thinking and feeling will multiply. So, in music what you are listening, writing, feeling, thinking, and add the physical part of singing and playing an instrument, will effect what you attract. You can literally attract what you want from the universe through song!

Whether you do this for money, therapy or fun, songwriting takes time and some amount of tenacity to wander your way through the art of songwriting and then to promote, submit and network your way to where you want to be as a songwriter. It doesn't matter how long it takes for you to get to where you want to go, because in songwriting, it's all about the process of writing your song. If you write one song, I hope your true passion and purpose find their voice.

Write for Yourself:

At first you should write for yourself. Write what you know, because then it will come across as being organic; the feelings will be real (I'm really good at this). Use your fundamental feelings as a foundation for your music. Songwriting can be very therapeutic by releasing your hurt, your anger at something you might not want others to hear, but let it out anyway. You may feel very vulnerable at first, but just keep writing. Start using metaphors (a word or phrase that is applied to an action or object that it is not usually known for), allusions (an indirect or passing reference) and personas (a different character) to take you out of the story. So, for your first couple of songs you may not want others to hear.

I love to write personal songs like my idols, Joni Mitchell and Pete Townshend, but even they consciously tried to write songs for the masses. Joni Mitchell wrote, "You Turn Me On (I'm A Radio)" specifically for "repositioning herself onto the Top Forty playlist."[9] Pete Townshend wrote, "Pinball Wizard" for the rock opera Tommy to please "influential UK rock critic Nik Cohn (who) was coming to review the project."[10] Although I like the "hit" songs, I love the personal songs; at least the ones I can relate to.

When writing personal songs, be careful not to get too personal. To quote Joni Mitchell again, her songs "are honest and personal based on the truth, but I exercise a writer's choice to change details."[11] To change what really happens is a good way for you to give yourself some distance from the story. Sometimes when a song is too close and personal it makes it hard to perform the song and it also could make your listeners uncomfortable. Not everyone will know that the story you're telling is not the truth. That happened to me. I take liberties with my stories and so a friend of mine thought I was talking about them. This was not good because they got angry at me, but I told them it was only partly true. You'll never know where a song will take you. Sometimes you just have to go there!

At a songwriting expo, I heard one of the panel professionals say, "Most people don't like it when the songwriter is the victim." I partially agree. The current (8-9-11) top 2 on billboard are: Party Rock Anthem and Last Friday

---

[9]   Hinton, *Joni Mitchell Both Sides Now - biography*, 143.

[10]   http://www.songfacts.com/detail.php?id=1527

[11]   Hinton, *Joni Mitchell Both Sides Now - biography*, 121.

<u>Night</u> hmmm! Looking at the top <u>100 hits on Billboard</u>, there are some sad songs, but not hopeless, "feel sorry for me," victim songs (in popular music). If you want to write a hit song, there needs to be a sense of self-worth for the one who's telling the story. The song "<u>Easy To Be Hard</u>" from the musical "<u>Hair</u>" was a hit, but most of the lyrics talk from the third person format through most of the song.

When people gather to listen to music they want songs to lighten their moods. They would take a jolly sing along song or dance tune over a despondently sad song every time, but melancholy songs have their place too. A lot of the songs picked up for film/TV are really sad like "<u>You Lose</u>" by Pete Yorn featured in the TV show House. TV is great for introducing new music and using music that is melancholy.

Exercise 1: Find artists that inspire you. If you have access to the Internet, join a music online service like, <u>Reverbnation</u> or <u>last.fm</u>. These sites and most networking sites like Facebook and MySpace will give you access to new music. Your assignment is to listen to one new song a day.

Certain personal songs are like a massive valve oozing feelings of drama and tragedy. I wrote a song I never play live because I feel that it doesn't empower me. It's a beautiful song called, "<u>I Am Powerless</u>." But writing this song did several things for me:

1. It got what I was feeling out.
2. It helped me to pinpoint what I was feeling (also making the video did that too).
3. Once I pinpointed what I was feeling I could then change it.
4. Now instead of having the feeling of powerlessness nagging away at me it's in a song.

So, if you have a hard luck story write a song because writing about it will help you define it. Defining what you don't want will help you define what you do want. So, perhaps when you write a hard luck story, back it up with a good luck story! Or begin with the hard luck story that resolves into a good luck story (maybe this will balance out the scale for the "law of attraction")!

Exercise 2: Use your notebook: Get a dictionary or thesaurus and find words to describe your feelings and write them down in your notebook. Define what is troubling or challenging you with words and then on the opposite page you will write the opposite feelings in words. That's it! Just write the words. You can fill a whole page of words if you like.

Writing Partners:

If you have little experience in the music side of songwriting but you have a good sense of writing lyrics, then find someone to write with, but finding the right someone is not easy. You need to find a partner that will complement you. The creative process can get personal. So, find someone you feel comfortable with. However, sometimes it is good to have someone to set limitations on your personal story. Above all, you will need to find someone who is looking for a lyricist (most songwriters do both words and music).

The easiest way to find someone to write with is to get on the Internet and hook up with someone via Facebook, MySpace, American SongSpace and Craig's List. You can also advertise at your local city college, adult education or music store by posting a flyer with your name and phone number. Also, attend music conferences put on by songwriting organizations (look at some of the websites I have listed at the end of this book). In addition to learning from this book, you could also take a course in songwriting at your local city college or adult education. These are ways to find other songwriters.

You can even partner with someone who is not from your town, state or country, but this can only be done (easily) via the Internet. Internet sites like <u>Soundcloud</u>, make it easy to send large files of music to another person or some people use <u>zip files</u> that condense the files when sending large files. There are other ways to send and share music but you can discover them on your own.

There are songwriters who partner all the time. <u>Steve Key</u>, a singer/songwriter friend of mine, told me that in Nashville it is very common for songwriters to get together to write songs. And so you hear, "let's get together and write a song sometime." It's like getting together for lunch or a drink. This is true, because I attended <u>Durango's Songwriter's Expo</u> in Santa Ynez California and met a bunch of songwriters from Nashville and they asked me if I wanted to get together and write a song with them! Ha! It's true!

Touring with another band:

If you're a good musician you can find a touring band to play with. A lot of time they'll be looking for singers or extra players. My nephew plays horn for two bands, Mad Caddies and King City. He met his first band in college and the other through musician friends and his reputation for being an awesome horn player (http://www.jenadouglas.com/music.html listen to "Walk On By" and "Again Someday"). So, usually you'll need to know the band personally. This is also a great way to see if touring is something you'd like to do for your own music.

Rock Star:

It is doable but you have to truly believe! And you have to really want it. Think about it, Paparazzi eww! However, you don't have to be rich and famous to make a good living from music.

Write Jingles for local TV and radio:

As long as you're up for the challenge, writing jingles and songs for commercials is a great way to get your style of music heard. From there, you can build your reputation, which for a jingle writer, is very important. Your reputation functions somewhat like a resume. "I wrote a jingle for this company, you may have heard it on the radio/TV." Usually, if you've got one song on a commercial and it does well you'll get regular work.

Write songs for famous singers:

To write music for famous singers is difficult because you not only will have to write in their style, but you also have to have a good singer to sing it. If you want to go this route and if you don't have a lot of money, my advice is to hire a good singer, or get some singing lessons. In Book II, I will go over some vocal techniques that I have learned through the years. This will help with learning to sing on key and how to strengthen your voice and broaden your range. Working on your voice will not only make you a better singer, but also make you a better interpreter of an interesting melody because your vocal range and pitch will then be better. Of course, there are singer/songwriters who have a small range and do very well.

Write songs and scores for film and television:

In "Change The World-Write Your Song! Book II," I will get more in depth on writing for this market. However, there are a lot of film and television shows out there that have singer/songwriter style music. A singer/songwriter can be just voice and guitar/and or piano, but make sure you are in tune and it is the best recording you can get. You must sound professional (unless you know who you're submitting your demo to). The do's and don'ts in the studio will come in my next book.

So, what you want to do with your music is totally up to you but at least you will know some of the options you have as a songwriter. The most important thing is that you become comfortable, fluent and inspired. Why don't we start by writing your song and then go from there. You may surprise yourself. Who'd have thought that with a few encouraging words and lessons, you'd be the next Dave Matthews or Jewel? Speaking of Jewel, she is the host for the TV show, "Platinum Hits." It's a show that is a competition in writing hit songs. This will help if you are interested in learning what music professionals look for in writing hit songs (Tip: great lyrics!).

In the next chapter, Finding yourself—"To everything there is a season," I explain the perks of songwriting and ways to find your inner songwriter. You will have the opportunity to realize what kind of music inspires you and what you want to write like. This first step introduces you to yourself as a songwriter. Who are you as a songwriter? Now, you've got to start to thinking like a songwriter. You've got to immerse yourself into your local songwriting community. Don't hurry, just enjoy the ride!

Highlights

What do you want—"We want the world and We want it . . . now!"

- Be yourself and play to your strengths.
- Know what you want and write a song about it that will attract it to you.
- Personal songs are great, just don't get too personal.
- Negative songs will bring more negative things to you by "law of attraction."
- But defining what you don't want will help you define what you do want.
- Most people want to hear upbeat songs in public!
- Film and TV are places to submit sad songs.
- Find a songwriting partner that challenges you.
- Better singing can produce better melodies, so take vocal lessons.
- Watch the TV show "Platinum Hits" for tips on what music professionals look for in a song (tip: Great lyrics).

Finding yourself—"To everything, there is a season"

"To everything, turn turn turn, there is a season, turn turn turn" I grew up to those words (adapted by Pete Seeger from The Book of Ecclesiastes). Of course, I remember The Byrds version of this song the most but the meaning is the same. There is a time for everything. So, don't try to hurry. That is my suggestion to you in finding your inner songwriter. Don't be in a hurry. Enjoy the ride! You'll learn that some people are born with a real sense of purpose and they just go from one happy little checkpoint to the next, checking off all the things that they are meant to do towards achieving their purpose. And then there are people like myself. Who love to do everything and can't focus on any one thing! There are no checkpoints for a person with no direction. I just went with the flow. The only thing I knew for sure was that I love music and knew a lot about what I didn't want to do. I guess that was a start. So, where are you starting?

I don't know what level of songwriting you are at. You may have written a few songs and just want a little reinforcement or you're just at the stages of, "I think I want to write a song," but be warned, songwriting is addictive! With every song you write, you'll feel like you're on some perpetuating spiritual quest. Songwriting makes you want to keep trying to write *that* song, *your* song, with all the right words that will be good enough to make the world smile! Come on! The world needs a smile and a nice big hug (yep, I'm a tree hugger)! What you get as the songwriter is the satisfaction of writing it! You get the buzz (happy feeling)!

A part of the buzz you get from songwriting comes from the "tension and release" of the songs' emotional flow. What I mean by this is that tension is the feeling of conflict in the song or story and then the release is when that conflict is resolved. After finishing a song you will feel happier with all those little tensions gone! Just like that. All you have to do is to write the song! It is important to keep writing and examining your feelings because what you might have felt one minute may change by the time you finish the song. When I write a song because I am upset about something the feeling is usually resolved by the time I've finished the song. So, the song finishes on a positive. And that is songwriting therapy! So, where does a song idea come from?

It is said, to write what you know, but sometimes that can be boring. That's when the fun comes in. As a songwriter, you can be anyone. You can be that person that everyone falls in love with or you can be a dragon with boots on. You can also write about the topics of the day, like world peace (this will attract more)! Whatever you want to be, it has to be something you are comfortable with writing about (if you're playing it in public). Always be true to yourself. What I mean is to use your feelings like a Geiger counter, detecting what's real in song. If it doesn't feel right, don't do it. As you gain experience writing it becomes easier for you to put what is being felt into words. You get quick at defining emotions and feelings for the story of a song. You become a better writer; you become a better "storyteller." What's your story?

Each idea for a song can come from anywhere. As humans, we write with our senses in full bloom. Whether we do it on a conscious level or not, we write what we feel through the experiences in our lives. We may hear, and be inspired to write songs from "within" as well as from the extremities like: a bird singing, a passing car or even a short musical line heard on the radio. I often start the songwriting process by listening to the styles of music I want to write like, but the muse speaks to me from a place I know not where? I just have to be relaxed enough to listen.

In this chapter you'll begin the process of finding your inspiration and creating yourself through song. For me, it's listening to music. I especially love to play along with songs that inspire me. I also get inspired attending concerts. When I was studying music at school I had to attend a lot of concerts and then had to write about what I heard. I don't know what type of music you like but it's a good idea to get to know how to describe the music you like.

Exercise 3 a: GO TO CONCERTS! SUPPORT LIVE ENTERTAINMENT!
Go listen to a singer/songwriter at a house concert or club near you. Check these sites out for a house concert near you http://www.houseconcerts. us/ or www.concertsinyourhome.com/. Choose an artist you want to write similar to. Getting to know the people in a concert setting is an important part of networking! In order to be known, you have to be seen. Plus, you can learn a lot about what you want to do with your own music. Do you want to be a performer?

Exercise 3 b: Use your notebook: Write about what you see and hear. Think like a music journalist. Compare the artist's performance to times you've seen them before. Is the artist playing with a full band, duo, or are they playing a solo gig? Do you know any of the artists that are in accompaniment? Does the artist sound like any other artist? In your opinion, could any of their songs be a potential top ten hit? If so, what song? What is their strong point, vocals, lyrics, music or guitar style? For fun, check out any review the newspaper had (if any) on the performance.

Artists "live" performances naturally sound different than their recordings because of things like the acoustics or alternating band members. Depending on your budget, you could have a different band playing with you every night. Solo artists such as <u>Caroline Aiken</u>[12], come into town and have a dozen people dying to play music with her. Her voice and guitar are amazing and it's fun to see whom she will put together for the gig. So, it's really hard to judge a "studio" recording against a "live" recording.

You, as a songwriter on assignment, are really there to observe the artist, to network and to study the audience (see what the fans are enjoying). If you really enjoyed a songwriter, buy their CD! or at least get on their email list!

Exercise 3 c: Use your notebook: After seeing several concerts, write down any songs that stood out for you. Try to find out what genre the songs you liked fall into (hint: go to band websites). Match up the songs you heard to each other and to the <u>current top ten singles</u> or more fairly to <u>music performance videos</u>. What do they have in common?

As a singer/songwriter it is important that you have interesting lyrics. I have hinted before that what most music professionals look for in a song are great lyrics. In the next chapter, I will assign some exercises for writing lyrics, but it is up to you to make them interesting and unique. I will give you all the tools for finding different ways to say things, but you will need to listen to your inner voice, your muse and to look at what makes a lyric good!

---

[12]   Aiken, Caroline. <u>http://www.carolineaiken.com/home.html</u>

Highlights

Finding yourself—"To everything, there is a season"

- You need to be true to yourself.
- To find your inner songwriter, don't be in a hurry.
- With songwriting comes the "tension and release" of the songs' emotional flow.
- As a songwriter, you can be anyone.
- Ideas for songs can come anywhere, anytime, so carry a portable recorder.
- Go to concerts and keep a musical journal.

Writing Lyrics—"From Your Fire"

"From Your Fire" is a title for a song of mine and is another way of saying, "From Your Passion." Lyrics are the most important part of songwriting. I cannot stress that enough if you plan to make a living on songwriting. It is a lyricist's job to say something familiar but in a different way. You will need to find the passion in becoming a wordsmith! A wordsmith is someone who is fascinated with words and likes to learn all the intricate and meaningful ways to rhyme and piece together words. It's like a puzzle that follows a melody to a story line. Being a lyricist is a never-ending fascination with words. It's an ongoing process of finding words and their meanings. The fun never stops!

The place you get the words to write your lyrics is implanted into your brain from years of listening and reading. It's like a memory muscle especially for writing words. And the more you use it the more of it will be available to use. That doesn't mean that you'll be writing hit song after hit song; it means that you will have the tools in your head to summon the right words for the story, but be prepared for the hit!

What I mean is, songs come to you differently, some you have to work at, some will sit around for years gathering in piles of rumpled paper not getting finished and some songs will hit you blindsided, "Pow!" And these "hit songs" (get it?) just seemingly come out of nowhere. So, be ready. What I'm saying is, a song doesn't have to be certified platinum (an RIAA award) to be a hit or to hit you! Look out! Here comes your song!

Where songs come from is the mystery of songwriting and like Leonard Cohen says, "I don't know where the good songs come from or else I'd go there more often."[13] You will write lots of songs and you'll write lots of good songs, but sometimes there will be a song that will come to you in a flash, like it was sent to you from a higher power. And when that

---

[13]   Zollo, *Songwriters On Songwriting*, 345.

divine moment comes, it will feel like the breath of an angel whispering in your ear. I know; I've felt it!

Songwriting is very satisfying, but with the divine intervention aside, it is sometimes hard to get the words to come out right, but I don't think there is ever a point where you feel you have all the words you will ever need (I'm still looking!). Build that memory muscle and do the research. It can be fun! And with regular use lyrics will come faster and easier.

Exercise 4: Increase your vocabulary! Read books, do crossword puzzles, memorize a word a day from the dictionary, read poetry.

Much like yoga, songwriting is a physical and metaphysical (or spiritual) discipline. Meaning, when you are singing or playing an instrument you are physically using your body to go with the beat and you are metaphysically feeling it through your senses when singing or playing the melody. In songs that have words, the lyrics pinpoint feelings being felt by the songwriter. By having a large vocabulary (or using a thesaurus) you can define your feelings many different ways.

Exercise 5: Use your notebook: Remember Exercise 2 when I had you write all those words? If you skipped that exercise here's your chance again. On the left side of your notebook write all the words to describe your feelings (use a thesaurus and/or dictionary), it could fill up a whole page, but just keep letting it pour out. Don't worry about lines or spaces, just let the floodgates open! Now, on the right side of the notebook, write the opposite of what you are feeling. Just let that flow! You should have words that directly conflict one another; perfect for writing a story.

To be a prolific songwriter is to be true to the feeling of the story that you are describing. To achieve this you've got to first define what you're feeling in the story and then use the right words to express that feeling. From those words (your words) you'll have to create your own rhyming scheme! It's your story, with your words and now they need to rhyme.

Writing rhymes:

Where would we be without a song that rhymes? Sure there are songs that don't rhyme but can you remember any of them? If you do, you are among a small percent because songs that are in verse and rhyme make it easier for the listener and singer to remember the song. Beginning in the middle ages, Troubadours traveled from town to town, singing songs in verse with rhymes that told stories of courtly love and the latest news of the day. Although you can trace poetry, rhyme and music back to ancient Greece, it is the Troubadours who cultivated meter and rhymes[14] that paved the way for popular songs, "Provencal troubadour movement, (was) the first spark of modern lyric-based music."[15] To understand this you must understand rhymes.

Perfect rhymes are used the most but you need to be careful not to be too predictable. The rhymes in a line or stanza (more than one line) need to sound new and unexpected. I like what David Byers says, "A rhyme works best when it seems like it was an accident that the words rhyme and the words are so fresh that we don't even notice the rhyming."[16] Hit your audience with a new way to rhyme with your words!

Perfect rhymes (also called, exact rhyme, full rhyme or true rhyme):
An example of a perfect rhyme would be: park and lark. With a perfect rhyme the consonant following the rhyming vowel is the same. In this case the vowel "a" in both park and lark have the same "r" consonant.

Near rhymes (also called, assonance and imperfect rhyme):
Near rhymes are like: fight and hind. With the near rhyme the consonant "g" and "n" following the rhyming vowel "i" are not the same. With a near rhyme, there are lots of possibilities. For one thing you completely ignore the consonants and focus on the vowels.

---

14 http://www.medieval-life-and-times.info/medieval-music/troubadours.htm

15 http://www.webexhibits.org/poetry/explore_21_song_examples.html

16 Byers, *Songwriting fundamentals discover the true joy of songwriting!* 43.

A **Masculine near rhyme** is a one-syllable word that rhymes the vowel at the end of the word. Example: race/late

A **Feminine near rhyme** is a two-syllable word that will rhyme on the stressed vowels as well as the unstressed vowels. And the unstressed vowel will come at the end of the word. Example: running/sunning.

There are plenty of different types of rhymes: wrench, syllabic, mosaic and consonant rhymes. Each will define the vowel's relationship with the consonant and what letter is stressed in the word. You can get lost in the technical ways to rhyme. My suggestion is to find the words you want to describe in your story and whatever you and your muse come up with, will be fine.

Here is an example of a mosaic rhyme and what might be a feminine near rhyme. When I write I don't think about the rhyme, I think about what sounds good. Rhymes don't have to come at the end of a word, line or stanza. They can come anywhere the meters of the words are stressed and they can come in multiple places along the line. For example from my song, "Boy:"

Line one:
   "Boy, start your running, cause I'm feeling something" (feminine near rhyme?).

Line two:
   "Boy, come to me closer cause I need a dose of" (sounds like dos/ sof) (mosaic rhyme) (this also is an incomplete sentence that is completed with the first word of the following line)

Line three:
   "Love that you keep to yourself, don't make me go out and find someone else" (another mosaic rhyme).

The more you work with rhymes the easier it is to find one. However, if you get stuck for a rhyme, I have provided definitions of the different rhymes in the glossary or you can use a rhyming dictionary. Here is one online (http://www.rhymer.com/). Important things to remember about rhymes are:

1. Find what letter or letters are being stressed, so you can find the right rhyme (except for a female rhyme is unstressed).
2. Find the right rhyme for the story.—Does it make sense?
3. You can be simple but don't be too predictable (simple/predictable = near rhyme).
4. How does the word sound in the song?—Is it too harsh sounding?

Listen to the word you choose to rhyme because, depending on how it's used in a song, words can be very harsh sounding. If a letter is going to be rhymed and you have a choice between an "ee" sound and a "oo" sound, I'd go with the "oo" sound because the "ee" tends to sound harsh especially when sung by an amateur. However, like in most everything I've said regarding songwriting, it all depends on the song and how you want the feeling played out! It is now your turn to tell your story. Just a couple more exercises if you want or dig right into your story. I know you're wanting to.

Exercise 6: Use your notebook: Take the words you used in Exercise 5 and find rhymes for them. This is your story you need to tell. You have the words, and the rhymes, now you need to have them follow a pattern.

Exercise 7: Use your notebook: In songwriting, there are different rhyme patterns. A popular way is to rhyme every other line, ABAB. Many of Bob Dylan's songs are written this way. In your notebook try different types of rhyme patterns. Write them in your book like from my song "Again Someday":

A—I'm just getting by
B—but the wheels are turning
A—I tell you no lies
B—When I feel something burning

Here are some rhyme patterns to pick from. You can do them all or just go from the gut (That's what I usually do):

A, B, A, B, B, or **A, B, B, A** or **A, A, A, A** or **A, A, B, B**

Exercise 8: Use your notebook: Now that you have the words and their rhymes for what you are feeling, and the words and their rhymes for the opposite of what you are feeling, write about the conflict of feelings using a rhyme pattern.

Lyrics can also create "tension and release" like what you learned in chapter two when talking about the buzz you get from songwriting. It is also a term for what happens in music (the melody and songwriting structure). Tension becomes the climactic part of the song (usually middle of song), while the release of the song comes from the resolve of the music and words. Resolving a conflict can be about anything. It can even be about getting the jar of peanut butter open. Conflict is what makes the story and lyrics interesting.

Writing lyrics is about telling a story. The most realistic story is a story about you. This does not mean that you have to tell the whole truth and nothing but the truth. No way! Paul Simon says,

> "If something from my life works, I use it. If I have to change it and exaggerate it because that works, I'll change it and exaggerate it. I'm not committed to telling the truth. I'm committed to finding what the truth is in the song."[17]

So tell us your story! I personally love an embellishment on a story, but make sure you stick to your subject. Don't let the horse go wild. Grab it by the reins, because you are telling a story you want everyone to understand and remember. Talk to the listener. Tell them what is going on in a way that they will remember. Use a few simple words and not too many syntactically long words and verses. It is common knowledge to write in verse (arranging words with a metrical rhythm) and in verse you have to use words that you would not regularly use in speaking. So, use colorful words and images that will express your state of mind. Just write and write and write! This is where you will find your own style. The character of the story will flow with the words you choose. If you're a visual person like me, it's easier to visualize the moment and then paint a picture with your words.

---

[17]   Zollo, *Songwriters On Songwriting*, 104.

Exercise 9a: Use your notebook: Write about a painting or photograph! Find the picture that tells your story and write your story. Don't worry about writing in verse, just describe the picture and tell its story; your story. You may have a picture at home that catches your eye and is begging for attention! So, write about it. "Every picture, tells a story, don't it"

Exercise 9b: Use your notebook: From the picture you've found, pick out three words that you can use as a metaphor, or simile (like a metaphor only you use "like" or "as") to represent a feeling or person. Be careful of what word you use, you may be stuck with a cliché. For instance, the word "blue" to represent a feeling has been done! Be creative. Use your notebook to write and rewrite if you have to. This is very important!

Exercise 9c: Use your notebook: Now take one of those metaphors or similes and use it in a verse. Follow it with an embellishment. The flower represents a person of whom you have some romantic involvement with. That is a metaphor. If I said, "you're like a flower" that's a simile. Now, use your notebook and write and rewrite your metaphors, followed by their embellishments.

Example:

> **1st part of line with Metaphor:** "I held hands with a *flower*,"
> **2nd part of line embellished:** "that blossomed and perfumed."

Exercise 10: Use your notebook: If you can't find a picture to write about, bring out the artist in you by drawing/painting a picture of your own. This is a good way to get ideas for songs and a great outlet for self-expression and discovery. So, paint a picture and choose a color for the way you feel and use it in your song. An important part of being a songwriter is writing what you visualize and sharing it with your listener. Nothing is more powerful than visualizing your song. Make your ideas heard with pictures! Describe the picture in your story; your snapshot of the moment.

Exercise 11: Use your notebook: If you can't write about something personal, think up a cool persona by reading an article in a newspaper or magazine or by watching a movie (good practice for writing to film). I love Elton John and Bernie Taupin's song, "<u>Indian Sunset.</u>" Can you guess the persona? Wow, what a powerful song! And you know, Bernie Taupin used his writer's privileges in this story of the Native Americans, but wow! Who cares? Right? So, write about your character.

When choosing your words, not only do you need to think like that person but you need to feel like that person too. With this little exercise you can escape the doldrums of everyday life and literally know how it feels to be someone else.

Two reasons to write a persona piece:

1. An escape from boredom.
2. Empathy for another person.

Write down on paper or carry a small recording device and "as that person" record any ideas you get from walking downtown, doing chores, hiking or seeing old friends. I can't tell you how many times I wish that I had a recorder. Ideas are here and then they're gone! You can also use the words (with their rhymes) you have from Exercise 5 for your story or make-up some new words.

Exercise 12: Use your notebook: Still can't write about yourself? Find a quotation and tell the story behind that quotation. Find out the Who, What, When and Where of the story. For inspiration and ideas, I sometimes look at verses from a favorite poem. Poems give us insight to a language that makes lyric writing interesting. You can get ideas and inspiration from reading poetry or I have also used, but not very often, quotation books.

Poetry? Quotation books? Seriously? Isn't that plagiarism (to take the work of someone else and pass it off as your own)? Well only if you steal the words and melody. I only want to get ideas, like how a certain word is used, so that I can write a story. Of course, be careful not to plagiarize.

Exercise 13: Use your notebook: Write a Holiday song or write about a day in a week. The media are always looking for these types of songs to promote. Think "Monday, Monday." Every week, writers, publishers and recording artists get a check for every time their song is played.

Exercise 14: Use your notebook: Streamlining is a great tool when writing verse. Look at Bob Dylan's tune, "Subterranean Homesick Blues." He seems to just ramble on with rhymes at the end of every line. Interpretation of the song can be different depending on a person's ideals, along with their environment and feelings. In a song, you have to make the feeling come through, regardless of whether it makes sense. It can be a Novelty song (ex. Purple People Eater). So, making sense of a song is not as important as keeping the feeling and rhythm of the words going. Of course, some will argue that every line must make sense and if you're writing for someone else that may be true, but for our purposes don't worry about that. Just stay focused on your story by completing the feeling and idea for the song. In your notebook, empty your thoughts onto pages.

Exercise 15: Use your notebook: Another thing that Bob Dylan did so well was to write to a person in a speaking voice. For example, he wrote, "You got a lot of nerve to say you are my friend" from the song, "Positively 4th Street." In the book, *Songwriters On Songwriting* by Paul Zollo, Bob states, " . . . another way of writing a song, of course. Just talking to somebody that ain't there. That's the best way. The truest way."[18] This exercise is to write to someone. It can be a letter or it can be a conversation with a person. Use a thesaurus to find colorful words and write them down in your notebook. Find words that will satisfy your thoughts to this person. Paint them in your picture.

Exercise 16: Use your notebook: Fine-tune your words. Write and rewrite your words by singing them out! Follow the natural rhythm of the words. Ask yourself, "Are the words in my verse too long?" "Do the words tell the story?" You'll know if they're too long when you feel like you're spitting out words faster than you can think about them.

---

[18] Zollo, *Songwriters On Songwriting*, 79.

Think simplicity and efficiency. Count how many syllables you have in a line. Fundamentally, you want one syllable per beat, never using a multitude of syllables per beat, and "never say never!" I mean, where would we be without, "<u>Something in the way she mo-oves me</u>." I don't like to say never in music, because I can always be proven wrong! In modern songs, we defy rules all the time. As I've said before, in music it is up to you, but in this exercise, sound out every syllable in a word and draw a line through it. ex. contribute = con/tri/bute (it has 3 beats and the "u" in the last beat is the rhyming vowel).

Exercise 17: Use your notebook: With your rhymes ready, let's build a verse. Apply these rhymes, similes, metaphors and embellishments into a verse. Use your notebook and write and keep writing them out until you are happy with how it reads out. Say it out loud. Do the lines syntactically follow a beat or meter? Does the context of it make sense? Write more lines if needed. Make sure it completes the thought with the other line or it feels like it's going somewhere.

So, now that you've got some ideas or even some full verses written down, it's time to put them into some sort of songwriting form. In the following chapter, you'll learn about the different parts that make up a song, like what comes after the verse and how they work with each other. Most songwriters will use some sort of songwriting strategy. Stringing all the words together and putting them into some kind of format is like putting together a puzzle. All the parts have to fit, but putting them together is one of the most creative parts of songwriting. It's your picture; your puzzle; your song! So, let's put your Muse to work!

Highlights

Writing lyrics—"From Your Fire"

- Songwriting is a physical and metaphysical discipline.
- Say something familiar but in a different way.
- Your song doesn't have to go platinum to be a hit.
- Exaggerate your story if that works for the song.
- Use colorful words and images that express your state of mind.
- Write down as many words as you can that pertain to the feeling of your story.
- Use a thesaurus and a dictionary.
- Paint a picture with your words.
- Fundamentally, you want one syllable per beat.
- Think simplicity and efficiency.
- Use more perfect rhymes than near rhymes.
- Don't be too predictable in your rhyme choice.
- Soft sounding vowels sound better when sung.

Songwriting methods—putting the Muse to work

Let's put the Muse to work! In Greek, mousa (mousa means muse, and there were nine of them: Erato, Efterpi, Thaleia, Kalliopi, Cleo, Melpomeni, Ourania, Polymnia and Terpsihori) is a common noun that means, literally, "song" or "poem." The Muses, in ancient times, were Greek Goddesses who embodied the arts and inspired the creation process with their graces through remembered and improvised song, stage, writing and dance. Sometimes when an idea for a song pops into my head, I like to think that it is my muse at work. So, put your muse to work when you want inspiration. Inspiration is the seed, but songwriting is a work in progress.

Which comes first, the words, the melody or maybe both at the same time? Many will tell you; sometimes it's both the words and melody because the *scansion* (words having a pattern and rhythm) is like a melodic phrase (notes having a pattern and rhythm). Sometimes we'll hear just a melody. Paul McCartney used "Scramble Eggs," temporarily to remember a melodic line until he thought of "Yesterday." They scan the same. Beethoven's motifs are full of bird sounds taken from his daily nature walks. *The Victor Book Of The Symphony*, writes about Beethoven's love of nature, "To walk by himself in the woods, to sit in the crotch of a favorite tree and sketch his musical ideas, to be out of doors at every opportunity were to him the acme of happiness." [19] Whatever the muse manifests for us, we must then take that inspiration and turn it into a working song.

On writing melodies, The Beatles were masters. In 2000, Paul McCartney's "Yesterday" was voted the #1 Pop song of all time by MTV and Rolling Stone Magazine. When you listen to "Yesterday," the melody creates an ascending climax and then it descends back down. This kind of melody is what makes it such a powerful song. It grips you like a good

---

[19]   O'Connell, *The Victor Book Of The Symphony*, 83.

horror film and then brings you back down feeling all warm and cozy. This is called "tension and release."

I know that I have listed "tension and release" before in Chapter two and Chapter four but it is also a musical term to create a feeling of movement. "Tension and release" is created when the melody wends its way up by step to the climactic part of the song (tension), and then wends its way back down to the beginning (release). As you are ascending and descending, you can repeat notes, go down and up, but usually the melodic line's final destination is the keynote the song is in.

For example, "Yesterday, all my troubles seemed so (ascends) far away" "Now it looks as though they're here to stay (descends) Oh, I believe in Yesterday" (did a few leaps to make it interesting). I don't think Paul was dwelling on or even thinking about, the analytical view of the song when he wrote it. He just listened to his muse. You don't have to be a melodic master, like Paul McCartney, to write a song, or even to write a hit song. There are a lot of hit songs these days that don't have much of any melody and they do just fine, but I personally love a good melody.

If you like to write melodies, don't forget to engage the words by expressing or coloring them. I like to use a thesaurus. Let's say your word is, "down" you might want your melodic line to go down. I regret that I didn't do that for my song, "And I Fell." The line reads, "life can be so strange, you get up just to fall down again" and I leap to a higher pitch (note) when I sing the word "down." Ugh! My teacher, Dr. John Clark at Santa Barbara City College, told me to sing it down, too, but did I? No! Whenever I play that song live, I don't leap up on the word "down!" Listen—http://www.reverbnation.com/jenadouglas

Depending on why you are writing songs, it is important to grab the attention of the listener. In other words, your song must stop a listener in their tracks from the very start of your song. Usually, it is a short phrase of music (called a motif) in the intro, and repeats throughout the song. The intro and other parts of a song are described below. The verse/chorus format is the most common.

Verse/chorus format Of course songs are written in many ways (many of my songs begin with the chorus) but top songwriters will follow a fundamental songwriting format such as below:

INTRO: The intro is about 4-8 measures (a way of grouping notes) of instrumental music that contains part or "the entire hook." The instrumental hook is usually the same as the chorus only without the words.

VERSE: Each verse should start telling the story of the song. It is good to match your words with the meter of the song; each syllable for each note. Rhymes need to be consistent and usually they come at the end of each line or every other line (see Chapter 4 Exercise 7), but change it up once in awhile. The verse needs to create anticipation for the chorus.

CHORUS: The chorus explains what the song is all about. If a listener isn't too sure what the verses are leading up to, the chorus will clarify. Think of your chorus, or "hook," as being the answer to the question. Be simple in your chorus because you want your words to be easy to remember.

VERSE: Continue to follow the story of your song. Just like an essay written for school, you need to have an introduction, a middle of the story, and the conclusion. Stay on topic-don't get sidetracked!

CHORUS: This is where you have the opportunity to repeat your "hook," which should continue to emphasize your song's main theme.

BRIDGE: The bridge is where you create some variety and tension by changing your melody line, modulating to a different key, and/or adding a lead break for the guitar. In the bridge, it is important to keep it approximately 8 measures, with the music building into a crescendo, ending with a final chorus.

FADE CHORUS: You will end the song by repeating your chorus over and over and then gradually fade out or write an outro to end your song.

Exercise 18: Use your notebook: Now let's apply a format to your song.

If you want to get the attention of the music lovers and the music industry think up a clever title. The title can carry the whole song. It needs to explain the song's story or be interesting enough for people to want to listen. What was that song called? How many times have you heard a great song on the radio and could not find it by the title? Most of the time the title includes the hook. One of my favorite exercises when I was in school was to write from a title. I have written two songs from a title. One called, "I Know The Night" and the other is "Happy Hearts."

Exercise 19: Use your notebook: Think up a cool title for your song. You can use this title for the chorus or hook. Take your time. Come up with three alternate titles. You may use one of the titles for another song if you like. Woody Guthrie had books filled with potential song titles!

Exercise 20: Use your notebook: Take one of the above titles and begin your song with it. I have a few songs that start this way, "Hello, Hello" for one. Old time lyricists like Johnny Mercer, had a lot of songs that started this way, Moon River (music by Henry Mancini).

The melodic line, motif or hook:

This is what people remember about a song. And when written right everyone will be humming your song! The musical phrase includes the "hook." Think of the theme behind Darth Vader in Star Wars. That's what I'm talking about. It doesn't need to be instrumental. It can have words like, "all I want to do, is have some fun" as performed by Sheryl Crow (just to use one example). It's catchy (Gad what a cliché!). Here is when you really need a good hand-held digital recording device because the idea for the hook could come from anywhere.

Exercise 21: Go and write your motif. If Darth Vader's theme is dark and intense what does your theme sound like? If you are perceptive enough and in tune with your Muse one will come to you! Then sing it into a recording device. Use your theme for your next song. Perhaps it's with the title you just wrote?

The next thing to do is to learn an instrument! If you already know how to play a guitar or piano then you might want to skip the next chapter. Or if you play a guitar and want to learn piano, turn to the next chapter. Being able to play an instrument opens up a whole new world of music to you. It takes time to master an instrument but it doesn't take time to learn an instrument for the purpose of writing a song. So . . . turn the page!

Highlights

Songwriting methods—putting the Muse to work

- Words have a pattern and rhythm (*scansion*).
- "Tension and release" is created by moving the melodic line up to a climactic point and then back down.
- Top songwriters will follow a fundamental songwriting verse/chorus format.
- The intro contains part or entire hook.
- The verse needs to create anticipation for the chorus.
- The chorus explains what the song is all about.
- The bridge is where you change your melody line.

Learn an instrument—"I've got a Gibson without a case"

For those of you who are lyricists it is important for you to know something about music. Initially, I considered myself to be more of a lyricist than a musician, but that had to change. For one thing, I got inspired to play an instrument and then, when I learned other people's songs, I became a better songwriter.

Learn to play guitar and/or piano because they are best for songwriting. You can easily learn chords on guitar or piano and then write your melody over them. To write a song you should be able to sing the words and melody. If you don't have a great voice, you can play the melody on guitar or piano. Since this book is geared towards singer/songwriters, I will assume (yeah, I know the joke) you can sing. You don't have to be a great singer, not every songwriter is known for his or her great voice (Bob, I think you have a beautiful voice!) but it's important to sing in pitch or at least purposely off key (you never know where the Muse will take you!).

Also, when choosing your instrument, think about what you want to do with your songwriting. If you want to do a lot of touring, a guitar might be a better choice only because it's easier to "plug and play." The piano/keyboard is heavy and cumbersome and you will need a piano stand and seat. However, when I was in the "all-girl" rock band, "Wet Paint" I played standing up with a keyboard that I could strap on like a guitar, but then I was in a rock band with other instruments backing me up. As a solo artist, you should play the piano seated for ease of playing. When recording, you can do so much more with a piano. Piano is also my instrument of choice when reading music. It's all laid out flat. Plug a keyboard into a computer and you could have anything from drums to violins.

Below are some chords on guitar you'll need to know. Each vertical line on these chords are strings. The string to the left is the bass "E" string and following to the right are: A, D, G, B and then E again only an octave higher. Each horizontal line represents the frets on the guitar. The black dots are where your fingers go for each chord.

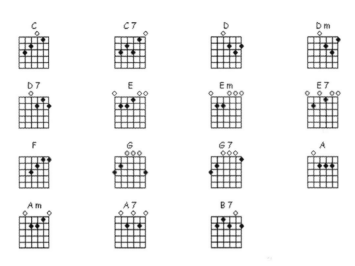

image provided by www.guitarchordsmagic.com

In order to play the guitar well, you must press down on the strings hard so the strings don't buzz. This will hurt, at first, until you can build up calluses on the tips of your fingers. Playing on an electric or nylon string guitar will be easier on your fingers. Also, have a professional work on the fret of your guitar to lower the strings. This is a good idea when you first purchase a guitar. Not only will it make it easer to play but also guitars often need work to make sure they stay in tune as you play notes up the neck. I always have the intonation checked on my new guitars. However, if you choose to play the piano, you don't have to build up calluses.

Below are pictures of chords on the piano. I have set up the chords according to a musical sequence used in theory starting with the tonic **I** (the key of your song), sub-dominate **IV** or **iv** (a chord used often in songs but not as often as the tonic or dominate chord) and dominate **V** (a chord that works with the tonic to make the song feel like it is going somewhere). In popular music you will hear all three of these chords being used. Use this chart as a tool for you in your songwriting. Notice the Roman Numerals being used. If you are not familiar with them don't worry. They are substitutes for the letters. Roman Numerals for a major chord are always in uppercase letters and minor chords are always in lowercase. Major = **I**, Minor = **i**, sub-dominate = **IV** (major key) or **iv** (minor key), and dominate = **V**.

To use this chart, first of all, pick your key. Do you want to play your song in a major or minor key (major = happy or minor = sad)? Then add the two other chords **IV (iv)** & **V** alternating them while singing a melody (Tip: going from "**V** to **I**" sounds like it's the end of the song. Also note that **V** is always a major chord regardless of what key you are playing in).

For example. If I want to write a song in A major:

- Find A major (**I**) on the chart
- Then scan to the right and use D major (**IV**)
- And E major (**V**) in your song

For A minor:

- Find A minor (**i**) it's next to A major
- Find D minor (**iv**) you'll have to search for it on the chart
- Find E major (**V**)

MAJOR I	MINOR i	IV (minor chord for minor key)	V
A	Am	D	E
B	Bm	E	F#
C	Cm	F	G
D	Dm	G	A
E	Em	A	B
F	Fm	Bb	C
G	Gm	C	D

(For the notes that don't show up on the black keys please refer to the piano scales and chord chart)

Using the Roman Numerals, here are some chord progressions that are useful for songwriting. Remember, you can start the progression of chords with any letter (key). Each slash is a measure (a measure is what breaks down the music into segments in this case it is the slash indicates the end of the measure). The double slashes are used to indicate the beginning and the ending of the chord progression. Count out each measure, 1 2 3 4 to yourself. So, you play **I** and count to yourself, 1234. Then you go on to the next measure and then the next and so forth.

// I / I / IV / I / V / I //

So, if you are in the key of A major these chord progressions will look like this:

//A /A /D /A /E /A //

Count in your head //1234 /1234/1234/1234/1234/1234//
12-bar blues looks like this in A major:

// I / IV / I / I / IV / IV / I / I / V / I / ii / V/ I //
//A /D /A /A /D /D /A /A / E /A /Bm/ E /A //

Count in head://1234/1234/1234/1234/ etc.

For now, all you have to know is that the piano chords will aid you in songwriting. You will learn more about Roman Numerals and their uses my second book, "Change The World-Write Your Song! Book II."

Exercise 22: Respect the masters of songwriting by learning song lyrics, chord progressions and characteristic licks from hit songs (it will make you a better songwriter). In your notebook, write down a chord progression from a song you really like and sing a different melody over the top of the chords. Record yourself while you are practicing (it will make you a better listener). You cannot copyright a chord progression but be careful not to copy the melody or words.

Learn your chosen instrument better by taking lessons. You can also teach yourself by picking up a book of your favorite songs and learn them. Also, I have conveniently provided scales at the end of this book. With these scales you can play leads over the progressions. You don't have to read the music because most songbooks will have guitar chords and you can play those on piano or guitar.

Learn how to use a drum machine or metronome. This will help you keep a steady pace. If you play guitar, make sure your instrument is in tune (electronic tuners are pretty cheap these days). Try playing your melody with your instrument of choice. Record yourself singing with your instrument. Listen to any problems you may hear with your intonation. Learn what notes you are singing.

Highlights

Learn an instrument—"I've got a Gibson without a case"

- Guitar and/or piano are best for songwriting.
- Singing the melody with your instrument will help you develop your ear and help tune your voice.
- Play to a drum machine or drum loops to help you keep time.
- Buy a tuner for your guitar and tune before you play.
- A song it must have a **I** and/or a **V** (a tonic and/or dominate).
- **I**, **IV** & **V**, are the primary chords used in blues and rock.
- Play a chord progression from a song you love and sing a different melody over the top.

A little theory can't hurt!—Ouch!

Reading music is something universal and is understood in any language. By learning to read music you can write out your music, making it easier for a trained musician to play your music. There is a lot to learn when you study music so, let's start at the very beginning and add things as we go. We will go over the fundamentals of music theory first. In my second book, "Change The World-Write Your Song! Book II," we'll go over more theory.

In written music there are notes and there are rests. The notes tell you when to play your instrument. The rests tell you when to be quiet. There are seven letters from the alphabet that are represented by notes, A, B, C, D, E, F and G. You are probably familiar with what a note looks like. You see them all the time on cards and music programs. Along with those notes are accidentals (sharps and flats). Accidentals have symbols that look like this # for sharps and b for flats. Sharps and flats are in between the lettered notes. For example: F sharp (F#) or B flat (Bb). How many accidentals used in a song will often tell you what key your song is in. Notes and accidentals are written on the lines or in the spaces of a musical staff.

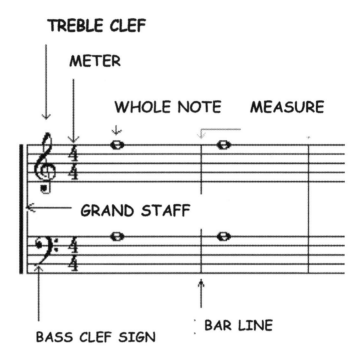

TREBLE CLEF

METER

WHOLE NOTE   MEASURE

GRAND STAFF

BASS CLEF SIGN   BAR LINE

The grand staff includes a bass and treble clef (sometimes an alto clef), Key and Time signatures (meter). The bars that run vertical across the staff line signify the end of a measure. A double bar line signifies the end of the song or section of music. Each measure has notes and/or rests in it, and when you play them, you make music. The clef tells you what octave to play your instrument. Most melodies are written with a treble clef like the one above. If there were any accidentals (sharps or flats) they would tell us what key the song is in. With no accidentals (like above) the song is in the key of C major or C's relative minor A (a clue is that the first note of the melody usually starts on the key the song is in). The time signature (meter) in the grand staff is the pulse of the song. It's the thing that makes you want to clap your hands.

To help learn where each note is on the treble staff, memorize this:

For the lines on the treble clef (from bottom to top) **E**very **G**ood **B**oy **D**oes **F**ine.
For the top treble staff spaces it spells the word **F-A-C-E.**
Without getting too detailed on music theory, the three most important components for songwriting are:

The time signature (meter) It is good to know the time signature of your song, so you can tell your musicians what the beat of the song is. Is it 4/4 time or 3/4 time? The 4 on top, is how many beats to the bottom number. And the bottom number represents the note being counted. So, 4/4 is 4 beats per quarter (1/4) note. 2/4 is two beats per quarter note and so on. See examples below. (The large C is the same as 4/4 time and a C halved is 2/2 time).

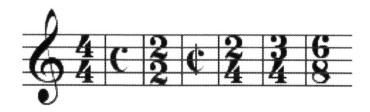

The Key signature: Learn the key signatures so you can tell your musicians what key your songs are in. This is very important if you are a singer. The circle of 5ths below will show you how many sharps or flats are in what key. It begins with the key of C that has no sharps or flats. The key of C is at the top and to the right is the key of G. If you count, C, D, E, F, G, that's 5 steps and so the sequence around the circle goes by 5ths. The circle of 5ths is exactly what it says. When I was in school, I made myself some flash cards with all the key signatures on them and I memorized them.

The circle of 5ths is also handy for songwriting. It is a great tool because you can learn not only the key signatures but also you can quickly see what the 5th your song is and what its relative minor is. The relative minor shares the same key signature as its relative major. Lots of times in songwriting we will use the 5th of a key for the chorus or bridge of a song.

The relative minor is the key you can also use in bridges and interchange keys for variations. For example: C major and A minor.

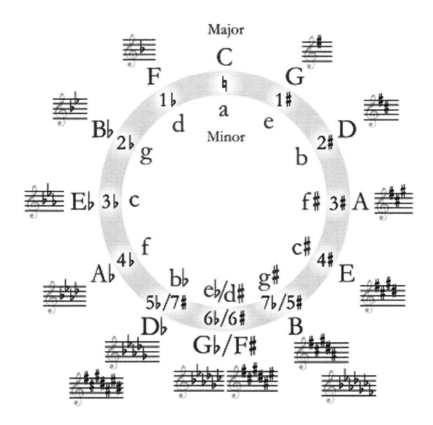

Chord Progression: As you have read in the chapter, "Learning an instrument," all music has at least an **I** and/or a **V**. Using the chart above will make it easier for you to find the **V** of any key you are playing in.

The best way to learn chord progressions is to learn songs that you like. After you have analyzed a song that you like, write a song using that progression. Don't worry about any copyright laws for using a progression; that only applies to melodies and lyrics. You cannot copyright a chord progression. You can also go and buy a book on just chord progressions but I find that learning songs I love, inspires me more. Word of caution, if you copy a progression from a song, steer clear of the melody! An easy way to do that would be to write your song in another key or different rhythm.

Counting: Notes and Rests

The first note value we will learn is the whole note. A whole note takes up one full measure and is held for four counts or beats if you are in 4/4 time. Count in 4/4 time out loud while holding down a whole note and say "one, two, three, four". When you add a Stem to the circle it makes the whole note a half note. A half note will get two counts. So, hold down the note on beat one for two counts then hold down on beat three for two counts. Then by filling in the circle, you end up with a quarter note. Quarter notes get one count each. So, for each note you count one, two, three, four. Next is the eighth note. Add a flag to the quarter note and you get an eighth note. To count the eighth notes in 4/4 time out loud we say "one-an-two-an-three-an-four-an" (you can say "an" instead of "and"). Finally, we have the sixteenth note. A single 16th note (not shown above) has two flags. To count sixteenth notes in 4/4 time, we say: "One e an a, Two e an a, Three e an a, Four e an a".

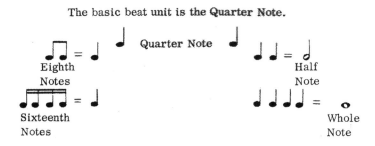

To be a singer/songwriter, you have to have a decent singing voice. Learning scales with your voice is just as important as learning scales for guitar and piano. Your pitch will be better and your voice will attain skills that will make you sound like a professional. In "Change The World-Write Your Song! Book II," I go over, in more depth, the best Vocal Techniques from acclaimed vocal instructors. For now, just make sure your throat, neck and shoulders are relaxed and do some vocal scales to warm up before singing. Do this daily!

Your voice is like any instrument; you have to learn to master your tunes and your tones. A good start is to massage your shoulders, your neck, your face and then your head. Then relax your throat by yawning. With the scales that you have learned on piano or guitar, start humming the scales with your lips slightly puckered. Your lips will tickle. Then, sing the scales. There are several different ways to sing a musical scale. One is to sing the notes of the scale. So, if you are in the key of C you would sing C, D, E, F, G, A, B, C and then back down the scale or you can use numbers.

Another way to sing without text is one I learned in school, called, the movable Do system. You assign a defined syllable to every note. This helps your voice achieve better quality and intonation. In the movable Do system, Do represents the tonic (root); the beginning note of the key you are singing in. For the key of C major and its corresponding notes it would go like this, Do, Re, Mi, Fa, Sol, La, Ti, Do. Teach your ear the intervals by learning to sing simple diatonic (only notes used in the key) songs; for instance: "Row row row your boat"—do,do,do re mi . . . etc. and "Three Blind Mice"—mi, re, do . . . etc. are examples of simple diatonic songs. It is possible to sing whole songs using solfege.

Try singing and playing the scale on the piano:

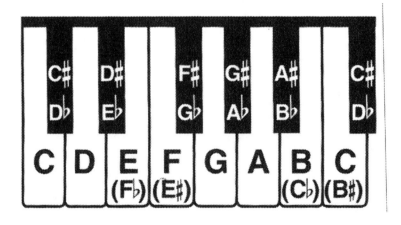

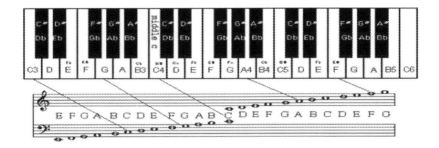

Or on the Guitar:

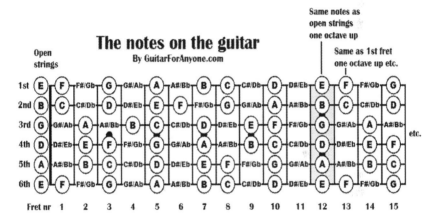

Image provided by www.guitarforanyone.com

```
o |-o-|———|-o-|———|High E string
o |-R²-|———|-o-|———|B string
o |———|-o-|———|———|G string
o |———|-o-|-o-|———|D string
o |———|-o-|-R¹-|———|A string
o |-o-|———|-o-|———|Low E string
    1    2    3    4
```

E | F | F# | G | G#|—frets top string

R^1 represents the root of the Key (in this case, **C**). If you are new to reading guitar tablature, imagine that you have turned the guitar upwards (so the strings [horizontally] face you). This, ironically, puts the top string (**E**) at the <u>bottom</u> of any standard tablature diagram. The strings that follow are **A**, **D**, **G**, and **B**, with the last string returning to E. The frets of the guitar start at the left and move up the scale to the right. From the E string, move fret by fret to the right (keeping in mind each fret is a half-step). Count the steps between each note starting with open **E**, then **F**, **F#**, and **G**. Play all the notes marked with an **o**. The capitalized **O**'s to the left are open strings.

To play the key of **C**, you want to begin with the root note on the **A** string (R^1). As you move up on the tablature, the next note you play is the open **D** string, then to the right the "**o**'s" **E** and **F**, play open **G** string and **o** for **A**, then open **B** string to R^2 (back to **C**). And that's the **C** scale on the guitar. Well done! You have learned two things; how to read tablature and how to play the key of C on the guitar! Remember this pattern because you can play around with other keys using this pattern, but what is most important is listening to the notes being played.

Get more scales from the Internet (<u>www.chordie.com</u>) and practice them. Try learning different scales like pentatonic and blues scales. Sing along with them to tune and develop your voice. I wish that I had done more of this before I went to school. Ear training was one of the hardest things I had to learn because I had never spent much time training my ear. If I had spent more time learning songs the "old school" way, I could have saved myself a lot of heartache. I performed quite well in music theory, but my ability to write a melody just by ear was really hard because I didn't spend enough time learning songs by ear. So, I highly recommend you singing along while you are learning scales and to learn songs by ear.

Highlights

A little theory can't hurt!—Ouch!

- The musical alphabet has seven letters: A, B, C, D, E, F, G.
- Notes and rests tell you when to play and when not to play.
- Learn what key and tempo you are playing in.
- Learn the circle of 5ths.
- Learn to sing without text with the movable Do system.
- Learn to sing a simple song in solfege.
- Sing scales with an instrument.
- Learn to read guitar tablature.

Creating art for the world—Showing your best side

Now that you've written your song, it's time to sing it out. The world needs to hear your voice! You are unique and sublime. And the world is in anticipation! So, write your little heart out! You now have the tools to write a song. So, tell us how you really feel about something! It is better to get out those feelings in song than to keep them all bottled up inside! Music is uniquely qualified to help you. According to the website, http://www.wfmt. info/WFMT/FAQ_Music_Therapy.html, music therapy helps:

> "Children, adolescents, adults, and the elderly with mental health needs, developmental and learning disabilities, Alzheimer's disease and other aging related conditions, substance abuse problems, brain injuries, physical disabilities, and acute and chronic pain, including mothers in labor. Source: Member Association AMTA, 1999".[20]

So, if your first few songs are of anger and hurt, so be it! It's all in the name of therapy! But then, it is my hope that with this book, you will eventually write songs that will fill the airwaves with positive emotions like love and peace! The world can never get enough love and peace!

To be a songwriter (or any artist for that matter), is to be a conscious observer of the world and how the world makes you feel, which is what you put in your song. You watch, you listen, and you observe what is around you. Writing a song will help you define how the world is affecting your mental state. When you realize how powerful words are when put to music you'll start to write songs that will draw feelings you want to have. And the world that is affecting you, positive or negative, will change.

---

[20] Heiderscheit, *World Federation of Music Therapy*, http://www.wfmt.info/WFMT/ FAQ_Music_Therapy.html

I wrote a song called, "My Life Is Gonna Change" (www.reverbnation.com/jenadouglas) and it did! Big time! I lost my job and moved out of town! So, be careful what you write for! Words and music together will make things happen. It can influence you and the world around you as the ripple effect of a pebble thrown in the water; your song will influence more than just what is around you.

So, as you start playing your songs out, start thinking of what your songs will attract to you, and how your song will influence someone else. If you don't like what you see in the world then write what you would like to see in the world. But before you go out and save the world, you might want to try your songs on your family and friends first.

This is a great way to introduce your songs and begin to master the art of performance. Unless you're a natural front person, performing can be really scary. With an adoring family watching, you can get used to the feeling of working your songs on an audience. By working your songs, I mean convincing them of your songs' purpose. In time, your musicianship, posture, and entertaining skills will become easier and you will be then ready for the next step. Having your family as your audience is a good beginning, but they will be biased. Playing in front of a group of people who think you could never do wrong will stunt your growth as a songwriter/performer, but it's a good start. In the music business you have to be tough and believe in yourself as well as your songs because not everyone will love you and/or your music. So, if this is too much for you? Don't stop writing! Just keep doing it! Try to find other songwriters who fall into your genre. Slowly, you'll start to realize that the songs you are writing are influencing the things around you.

There are plenty of friendly songwriting groups you can join that will support you and at the same time give you constructive criticism. You can find groups like this at your local Adult Education, City College or look online for songwriting groups in your area. A lot of cities will have groups that meet up for monthly song circles.

A song circle is when you and, no more than, ten songwriters sit in a circle and take turns playing songs. If you have more than ten songwriters playing songs in a circle, then you won't have the opportunity to play very many songs. Sometimes, if there are a lot of people, we will split into groups, but make sure you are out of listening range. I mean it can be distracting if you have one soft singing songwriter in one room and a loud (that's me!) singer in the other room. If your city or town don't have one, it would be easy to put a song circle of your own together. Ask around your town about other musicians and songwriters (hint: music stores + coffeehouses). Song circles are a great way to try out new songs and a safe place to perform. It's kinda like a party with a purpose! Everyone is asked to bring a dish to share and something to drink. Then you play music!

Also, find out if there are any open mics in your town. An open mic will get you and your music out there, and get you used to performing. All these things are great ways to find other musicians, other songwriters, promoters, and fans. You might even find other musicians who want to put a group together with you playing your songs!

Check out some of the websites I have at the end of this book. There are a lot of groups online. It can be confusing and overwhelming. A great songwriting group I know of is called, <u>Summersongs</u>. They have four camps yearly, two on the east coast and two on the west. I regularly attend the west coast group. It's the best community of songwriters and musicians I have ever met. I have made many great connections through this organization. It is well worth the expense, plus there are scholarships in case you're low on funds. You should also create a blog about your music. Blogs are a great way to get your name out there in cyberspace and they're free. The catch with a blog is that you have to blog at least 3-4 times a week for people to stay interested. <u>YouTube</u> is the best place to promote yourself. It is by far one of the fastest ways to get your music heard!

The next step is to showcase your songs. Once the songs are fine tuned, you can play them in front of songwriting critics. This can be a very rewarding experience or a very hurtful and disappointing experience. I've known people who have gotten very good comments and some who felt like they would never perform again. I do not recommend this for the weak at heart. On shows like, America's Got Talent, American Idol and Platinum Hits, you can meet other aspiring artists but I feel that if you lose it is like saying your songs aren't good and I don't endorse that. Songwriting competitions are good for promotional reasons but just because you didn't win doesn't mean your song is not good. I believe everyone has a song to share and I will endorse any songwriting competition where there are no losers but unfortunately that defeats the purpose of the competition. I think Art should be for Art's sake.

I know that ASCAP and BMI put on conferences that are open for anyone. At these conferences you can submit songs in person to music experts and they will critique them or you can attend the various scheduled panels of successful songwriters, who will share their secrets and tips for a number of songwriting related topics. Far-West, Folk Alliance, and Durango's Songwriting Expo, offer more chances to showcase your songs and you! By attending any of these conferences you learn a lot about your craft, but it's more in line with getting to know faces and them getting to know you. These conferences usually last for three days. You stay at the central hotel where everything is happening and it's very intimate.

Every year you see the same faces, it's fantastic! See if you can at least budget one in. Which one? Depends on you "doe nit." Check them all out independently to see what fits you and what you want to do with your singer/songwriting career (it's so worthwhile).

I recommend submitting your songs to anything that's for free; check out Hello Music it's currently free and NSAI (Nashville Songwriter's Association International) has a small annual fee and discounts for students. One of the things NSAI does for members is they give 12 free evaluations of your songs per year. This is totally worth it! Just remember, when you get your evaluation from any source, it's all about the listener's current frame of mind. To give constructive criticism is one thing but to downright tell you it's awful is another. I don't believe in that. Everyone has a song! Sometimes when you are submitting songs for film/TV or another artist, the music executive may know exactly what they are looking for. It's not about you, it's about fulfilling a checklist of styles and context of song an artist is looking for and it's not you. Take no offense, because you know your music is just that, your music, and you have so much more to explore! Don't stop, go to the next gig and then the next and keep going! If it's something you love doing, do it! No critique can harm you.

Keep a log of all your transactions during the day. Keep a log of all your submissions and know that you have to be selected out of a thousand submissions entered. Rarely does a songwriter get picked up, but there is the occasion when they will find what they are looking for in your music. The critic is usually a representative of a large publishing company that is looking for songs for their artists or they could be A & R representatives from a record company looking for new artists to pick up. You'll find showcases in large cities, which is unfortunate for many who live outside the city limits, but with the Internet you can still get your music out there. What you will need is a good recording of your song and video.

Record so that the world can hear! I love to record. There's nothing like writing a song and then recording it to see what it sounds like with all the instruments. That is when you hear your song in as perfect a form as it can be. However, it doesn't mean that your song is done. Sometimes it is best to play around with the song live before recording. Then sometimes you just want to re-record a song with a different style. Often, you'll hear a song sound different in the recording of a live performance. There are many songs I play one way now and then play them differently on stage.

Home recordings are inexpensive and are incredible sounding. A few good microphones, and a computer, and you're set. In "Change The World-Write Your Song! Book II," I'll discuss more on this, but for now you can make quality sounds with home recordings. It is important when you are an artist to have friends. They are assets because they support you in ways you could not do alone. If you're in a band, record the new songs after you have played them out. Give the band a chance to settle into your song. Unless you plan to go solo, you'll need a band. Look for potential band members at the local music stores, colleges, and the Internet (Craig's list is a good one). Show up regularly at an open mic in your town; you might find band members that way.

In the next chapter, "Smile for the Camera"—"I know they're gonna love it!" you'll learn about publicity, marketing and promotion. All this stuff is important if you're planning on making music as a living. If you get really good at marketing and promoting yourself, you'll find the people/fans who will want to help you. Helping hands are always welcomed when you're promoting!

Highlights

Creating art for the world—This is my best side

- Music is uniquely qualified to help you.
- Be careful what you write for ("law of attraction").
- Begin by performing your songs in front of family and friends.
- Master your performances by performing regularly.
- Join local songwriting groups in your town.
- Find other songwriters with similar styles.
- Organize your own monthly song circles.
- Showcase your songs to music professionals.
- Home recordings are inexpensive and sound great.

Smile for the Camera "—"I know they're gonna love it!"

What is publicity? What is marketing and promoting? To market is to find the "who" who will buy your product and the "where" to find them. To promote is to tell everyone you know what you are doing, where you are doing it and how he or she can find your music. So essentially, marketing is "the who" and "the where" (demographics) and promoting is the advertising, which will get your music to them. The best thing for a budding budget, star-struck musician is; publicity. If you're famous, you'll sell more CDs. Doesn't that make sense? How can this be done? I don't know, I'm still trying, but here is what I have been told.

First of all, identify your goals. Do you want to tour? Do you want to just play around town? Then, choose something to promote, like a CD release party and tour! Send out a monthly gig calendar via Internet. Make sure your social networks are up to date. Pick a date for the big event and promote; working all networks, including YouTube! What will you promote? Free stuff is always a crowd pleaser. A free download is always nice, but you know everyone does that . . . what will make yours different? What can you do that will catch the public's eye? It has to be unique, compelling and up to date. Publicity is free, but to get it you have to have . . . gulp . . . a gimmick, to suck the press in. You can try to get on "America's Got Talent" or "American Idol" for quick press, but those shows are not really geared for songwriters.

Make sure your website is up to date and interesting. A professional will look at your site and if it looks professional then they'll take a closer look. If you offer free downloads, that professional will be able to take your song home with them to listen at another time or for someone else! Promote your new love song for Valentine's Day by offering it free during the month of February. You'll need to have a story for the press. Be yourself but find your passion. That is always a winner! Voice your passion! If it's saving the dolphins or finding food for the hungry, sing it out.

When you get gigs, start with your city and work your music outward town by town. Working in your own town you have access to lots of talented people. You don't know until you start looking at what your immediate friends and family can do; someone who can design a logo, take pictures, videos and promote you. Being a part of a community college is a good resource. Take small quality steps and be true to yourself, be assertive but also be thoughtful and humble. Be approachable. People who come to see you are your customers; just like any business.

When you're ready to record and are short on cash, go to this online service, http://www.kickstarter.com to raise funds for your next project. I've had two friends who successfully raised enough money to do their recording projects. Once you have your recording done, you can build yourself a press kit.

Building a press kit: How well your press kit looks is important. Anyone in the music business will see a ton of press kits. You need to be different and you need to know who the press kits are for. Know what they are looking for. You are supposed to talk in the 3rd person, but I have read some compelling first person biographies. The heading to your press release bio is important. When giving a press release bio you need the following heading:

For Immediate Release   Name
date   Press Release/Bio

For more information about press releases and other music promotional tools check these sites: http://www.publicityinsider.com/release.asp and http://www.ehow.com/how_8793_write-proper-press-release.html Things change so it's best to just keep up via online. There will probably be a time when this method of promotion will be obsolete. But it's good to have all the information needed for the press.

When you get gigs lined up, you'll need to make posters. On the posters you will need: band name, date, time, place, style of music, any short quotes or news-press clippings about your music, and a picture of the band. Most software programs make it easy to make posters but if you can afford it, I recommend getting a professional to do the work for you. For a special event I recommend making a large, well designed, poster, 15" x 17". For smaller venues, a regular 8 ½" x 11" will be fine. Get these posters up at least two weeks before the event. For a special event, get your posters up a month or two before the gig. Put them up everywhere around your town: event boards and window fronts of stores. Don't forget the venue itself. After the show, don't forget to remove your posters. Also, make small handout posters to give to people so they can take them home as a reminder. Have your band members pass them out too. Don't forget anyone, but don't be annoying either. If you have a day job, make sure everyone knows when and where you are playing. For promotion on Facebook don't be too pushy or you'll lose friendships.

At your gigs, collect e-mail addresses by having a clipboard with places to write down their contact information (some people don't have access to the internet) and refer to it during your show. Promote your next show by leaving a small handout poster on each table and/or hand them out at the door.

Don't forget to get airtime on the radio. Research the radio stations in your area to find out if your music will fit their format of music. Make sure you know when to best air your songs. Like if the radio station has a local radio air show. Try pitching your songs to the smaller markets first. In other words, if you live in Los Angeles or New York pitch your songs to stations in smaller surrounding markets first. Send your press package to the stations' local shows or if they don't have a local show then send it to the music director. Also getting to know the DJs and program directors' assistants is a way to get your music on the station.

Interviews: When you get that interview "live" on the radio, make sure you don't forget to tell them where they can find your music, via your website, iTunes, CDbaby, etc. and where your next gig is. You'd be surprised how easy it is to forget when you're "live" on radio. If you're really prepared you can make up a three-minute bio. Just pick out the most important facts about yourself in three minutes. It's not easy to do! Bring the timer out and time yourself. If the radio station has a website, see if they can post your gig calendar and/or website address. When the media is interviewing you, you need to know the above information to fall back on but be prepared for anything, especially if it is "live."

After submitting your press kit to the local media make sure you try to get to know them better. You want someone from the media to promote your show. Getting a chance to play live on air is a great way to promote your show. See the paragraph on interviews above. Get yourself in print by inviting anyone from a local paper; offer them free drinks and dinner. The best way to get the buzz circulating is to get the local media talking about you. Also, the media needs to see how popular you are. So it is a plus to have a large following before you invite the media, but it doesn't have to be your following. You could be the opening act before a popular act.

Collect e-mails from everyone you meet that may be interested in seeing a show. Have an e-mail program that can send mass e-mails. Keep a file for press info on the shows and have it ready to include into your e-mails. You need to build a community around you at gigs and online. Blogs and online networking sites are a great way to get your name around.

Take control of your music. Don't wait for record companies to come to you. Go to them. Make it easy for them to find you. As a songwriter, you will need to build a website (Mine is $20 monthly or $199, yearly w/ Hostbaby. I know there must be cheaper hosts for websites. If you can't afford one, open a Facebook, Reverbnation and MySpace account, they're free. Reverbnation features pages for bands and their music, networking, emails, promotional work, a store for your CDs, etc. and you can also see graphs of how many people visit your site, what they listened to, etc. Great site! You should have a page on this site anyway (http://www.reverbnation.com/).

Make sure that all your web accounts look interchangeable with each other, meaning if one website looks like a pink fluffy girl site and your band's MySpace page looks like death metal on mushrooms (not really sure if I'd like to even think about this one). OK so that's a bit far fetched but you know what I mean. That would give a confusing insight to your music. It would say that you were not ready for any press release. Record companies today want to do less, so the more you have yourself together the better. They need to be professional and well thought out. Take a class at the local college on building a web site. Other web accounts you should get to know are located in the chapter below; Websites—People you need to know. Having success independently is the first thing a record label looks at other than your music.

Not everyone will like your music. That's just the way it is. Don't waste your energy on the "don'ts" but the "do's!" If you can compare yourself to an artist, you'll likely find people to buy your music. For example, "I have been compared to Sheryl Crow." Put this in your press release or if you're modest put down your influences. Find out what their genre is, and saturate that market with your music. That market will include a refined listener, journalist, and Record Label that is already receptive to your style.

Even if a record company is interested in you, make sure your music fits. What good will it do, if you get a record deal if no one listens to your music? Let's say you're a country artist. What good would a heavy metal record company do for you? Narrow your field and speak to similar acts with the label. Find out what successes they've had. Have your contract reviewed by a music lawyer.

Submit your songs each month via the Internet to film and T.V. music supervisors. Set a certain amount of money aside just for submitting your songs. Usual costs are anywhere from $2-$1000 (Be careful it could nickel and dime you to death!). I know someone who paid out over $2000 to Sonic Bids on various things, but he did end up winning "songwriter of the year."

Be business-like. You are being paid for a service. Make sure you maintain good relations with your fans and with club owners. Show up on time to gigs. Return e-mails. Stay in touch. Thank the people who buy your CD or tip you. Recognize them by being thankful for their support and for watching you! If you don't like doing this then get yourself a manager or stay at home and write songs.

If this all sounds like hard work, it is what you make it! You could record demos and solicit them to publishers, film, TV or record companies via Internet, but I highly recommend playing out because you meet more people who can advance your career that way; you can make more money; you can refine your skills!

In the next chapter you will learn about the music business. There are a lot of hats to wear if you are managing yourself. This chapter will go over all the different parts of the business of music. It's not my favorite part but then again most of the songwriters I know don't enjoy this side either. However, it is a good idea to at least know what the different facets are for the business of music.

Highlights

"Smile for the Camera"—"I know they're gonna love it!"

- For marketing you need to know "the who" and "the where" (demographics).
- For promoting it is the advertising which will take your music to them.
- Publicity is free, but to get it you have to have . . . gulp . . . a gimmick.
- Offer free downloads for a promotion.
- Make a video for YouTube.
- Use online service, http://www.kickstarter.com to raise funds for your next project.
- Know what the press is looking for when submitting your press kit.
- Collect e-mail addresses by having a clipboard at your gigs.
- Pick out the most important facts about yourself in three minutes.
- http://www.reverbnation.com/ great site to promote, network, sell, etc. and it's free.
- Make sure all your web accounts look interchangeable with each other.
- Maintain good relations with your fans, club owners and media friends.

The 'Biz—I'm too sexy for my hats!

As a singer/songwriter, and if you don't have a lot of money, you'll have to "wear a lot of hats!" Here are some of the "hats" an artist will need to wear. Below, I organized and explained each section to the music business with the help of Peter Sellman's book, *The Self-Promoting Musician-Strategies for Independent Music Success.*[21] I highly recommend it for anyone who wants to be a performing songwriter.

THE MUSIC—Repertoire • Rehearsals • Writing • Gear

Repertoire: Repertoire means a stock of songs that are ready to perform. You will need to provide venues and online music promoters a set list of the songs you play. A lot of clubs will want to see some familiar songs along with your originals, but not all. There is a lot of interest in house concerts and smaller venues that promote independent solo/band acts.

Rehearsals: Set up rehearsal times if you plan on having a band back you up. You will need to find a rehearsal space, unless you have great neighbors.

Writing: This is the songwriting part of singer/songwriter. You should always be writing. Songwriting daily will strengthen the songwriting muscle. Yep, just like any muscle, it needs attention!

Gear: Upgrade your equipment often. The better your equipment sounds the better you will sound. If you're a guitar player, get a good sounding guitar. You should have your own PA (public address) equipment.

PROMOTION/MARKETING—Planning • Media/Publicity • Distribution • Merchandising • Video

---

[21]   Spellman, *The Self-Promoting Musician*, 49.

Planning: Some events take months, and even years to plan for, just ask Renee Bodie of <u>Bodie House Concerts</u>, who puts on a pretty successful "<u>L.A. Acoustic Music Festival</u>" every year! A touring band would also need to plan (or not!). And then there's setting goals and planning the time to keep those goals.

Media/publicity: Publicity is by far one of the most important aspects to the business and success of any artist. Popularity gains fans over someone who you might think is better, but nobody likes him/or her. I did know someone who was very scary to be around but a phenomenal musician! True story. You have to stand out above the others, but you don't have to be brassy either (I'm thinkin' Jack Johnson). You need to be believable and true. You can be "the cutesy playful type" or be "the silent type," it doesn't matter as long as you have a good hook or gimmick (some may call it, I don't)! Be something unique in a "natural for you" way. Follow the feeling of the times. Be interesting! Create a catch phrase that describes you and your music. Be a spokesperson (Jack Johnson, Surfrider Foundation) for a non-profit.

Distribution: This refers to your CDs, DVDs, books, pens, t-shirts and belts! There are a lot of distributors online. I have included a few to start with on the websites page. Also, I read somewhere that now-a-days many record companies are just glorified distributors. So, that's great. I think!

Merchandising: CDs, DVDs, t-shirts, pens, and posters. You need to keep track of sales for tax reasons.

Video: Videos are used to promote on the Internet and are a very easy way to promote yourself. Study up on tagging yourself online or in my next book, "Change The World-Write Your Song! Book II."

RECORDING—Studio Research • Pre-Production • Production • Manufacturing • Record Labels

Studio Research: Finding the right fit for you is important. If you are not recording at home you will need to find a studio that will fit your style and budget. Some studios sound different than the others so, look around. You can't have too many options. One studio might sound really great for your softer sounding songs. While another studio might be just what "your little rock and roll soul" wanted with sounds that are "A little rough around the edges." It all depends on your CD and how you want it to sound. You don't have to be true to one studio. Usually, they will have recordings of artists they have produced available to listen to.

Pre-Production: Before you go into the studio you will need to have a idea of what you want your songs to sound like. If you have a band that you work with you should rehearse until you've got the songs "down." You don't want to be in the studio going over and over parts to a song; it'll cost you time and money.

Production: It's the producer's job to get your best sound, whether it's you or a professional recording it. Sometimes the recordings might entail beefing your sound up with lots of strings and horns and sometimes the song is told better when it's stripped down to just guitar and voice (with good microphones of course). That's what a producer should do, but not always. You should know that producers have sounds all their own and if it doesn't agree with you, you should find someone else. Some producers are famous for their own sound, for example Phil Spector, and his "wall of sound," produced The Beatles, Let It Be, album. Check out the differences in sounds between; Let It Be and Abbey Road. Big difference! Make sure you get involved with your sound. A good song is a good song regardless if it has an orchestra playing over it or it's stripped away to just guitar and voice. I hear a lot of singer/songwriters on TV with just a simple guitar and voice. So, keep that in mind if you're submitting to film/TV.

Manufacturing: The days of CD sales are almost over. Most people buy online now. So, don't spend a lot of money pressing 1,000 CDs when you really only need maybe 200-500 to start. You can always have more pressed.

Record Labels: Since CD sales are down; record labels are looking at different ways to make money with artists. It is still great to get a deal with a label, but so much has changed in this industry (and may change back again at the final pressing of this book!). Record labels don't put out a lot of money for acts, unless the acts have done most of the work. Meaning, the acts already have a lot of fans buying a lot of CD's and merchandise. At this point, you might want to think about starting your own label because you won't need a record label, you'll need a manager!

PERFORMANCE—Stage Show • Booking • Touring • Sound and Lights

Stage Show: Even a solo artist will need to put on a show. Even if it's just a great performance of their songs! Feeling comfortable in front of an audience enough to talk and make jokes is not necessary, but it helps. You need to be prepared musically. Impress them with your songs. Tell them your story. Let your passion out! Today you have big production performances by Elton John, Madonna, Beyonce, Lady Gaga and many others but in the beginning nobody is going to expect that from you. You just need to look confident, comfortable and be articulate about the stories in your songs.

Booking: Booking places to play is an important part of getting your music out there. Playing out will toughen you up as a performer plus you'll sell CDs and merchandise. When touring, booking your dates can be difficult. You might want to book your first date at your furthest destination (have the venue give you a couple of dates to work with, but don't wait too long to get back to them) and then work your way, from town to town, backwards to your starting point. After knowing your destination, book gigs on a different route back. Also, get alternate dates with venues in case your first choice doesn't work.

Touring: Plan to tour locally first, then spread yourself out. House concerts are very popular for touring musicians. Try these sites: http://www. indieonthemove.com/tips/ and http://www.houseconcerts.com/main. php. You can plan your routes around the gigs you find on the way to your furthest destination. Rachel Sedacca tours the country in her big renovated school bus. She does this thing she calls, "Dinner and a song." She finds friends via social networking groups throughout the country that want to host small dinner parties with Rachel as the guest musician. "Dinner and a song" is different than a House Concert in that it's smaller and more intimate. A musician will perform for dinner and a night off the road. Guests are encouraged to buy CDs and give cash donations for traveling expenses. Map out gigs along your route and with a few "Dinner and a song" performances, a few clubs and coffeehouses and you've got a nice little tour.

Sound and Lights: Having a good sound is important and knowing how to get a good sound is something that takes time. Most clubs have their own soundman and lights. As your own manager, you will need to make sure the club you are playing at has a sound system, a soundman, and someone to control the lights. This is especially important if you are recording or videotaping. Ultimately, you'll want your own soundman that knows how to get the best sound out of you; in any room! Often the soundman will also control the lights as well. This works, unless you have a big budget and a big show. Then, get the professional who's gonna know how to make you look and sound your best!

LEGALITIES—Licenses • Contracts • Insurance • Taxes • Trademarks

Licenses: In the music business there are a lot of licenses. As copyright owner you have legal rights to use your songs but if you use someone else's songs or someone uses yours; you will need a license. I will explain more about licensing later under licensing, UGH.

Contracts: There are many good books and online services out there on writing your own contracts, but before signing anything, get a good music lawyer. Make sure they specialize in the music business. Things change on a daily basis almost (well not really) and it would be good to get someone who is on top of the latest laws involving music and the entertainment industry.

Insurance: When a musician is on the road, having insurance is a must for your car, equipment, and for medical reasons. This advice is often not followed because of the costs, but well worth it. Insurance is especially important for a touring musician who is having car trouble, gets robbed or gets sick. My nephew Keith, while on the road with the Mad Caddies, has seen the benefits of having insurance. Stuff happens!

Taxes: You can do it yourself, but why? Make sure you keep good records of your expenses and all the money you make from sales and gigs. Also, at the end of the year, if you pay any band member over $600 to gig with you, you need to get a tax form 1099 for each member. You will need to get their tax information and give them a 1099 each for their tax returns!!

Trademarks: Band name or an individual performer is a trademark and should be protected. Also, a "word, phrase, sound or symbol that represents in the marketplace the commercial reputation of a product or service." [22] These are defined as trademarks.

BUSINESS—Planning • Office Setup • Resource Management • Networking • Publishing

Planning: As a business, you need to set up immediate and future goals. Have a one-year and a five-year plan.

Office setup: Just like any office you will need a computer and a printer/scanner for promotions and communications.

Resource management: To efficiently and effectively organize all your resources, such as; financial information, inventory of products, musician for hire, studios, production resources, or know about the latest information technology.

Networking: Returning emails, keeping current on your social pages like MySpace, Facebook, Twitter, YouTube and your own website. The Internet has made networking a lot easier and cheap! Joining organizations and attending parties (somebody has to do it!) is all a part of networking.

Publishing: Whether to publish your own songs via BMI, ASCAP, and SESAC or to submit songs to publishers. This business side of music is not to discourage you from songwriting. It is unfortunate that the hard, cold, facts of business come with such a creative thing as songwriting. Perhaps this is the time that you decide to just keep songwriting a hobby, but if you love music and want to make a living at it, you'll do anything. Try to organize your days into: **Monday**—office and legalities day, **Tuesday**—Promotion/marketing days, **Wednesday**—music rehearsal day, **Thursday**—recording day, leave **Friday**—**Sunday** performance days. Just an example of how you can fit it all in. Of course, I spend a lot more time writing than anything else, but I do try to stick to some sort of order. I also have to

---

[22] Wilson, *The Business and Legal Guide for Songwriters and Performers Making It in the Music Business*, 231.

fit in household stuff like laundry or fitting a card game in with my family.

LICENSING! *UGH!* They can be exclusive or non-exclusive.

Licensing is, the sometimes confusing and ugly part of songwriting, but "now a days" it's really pretty darn easy. You can take care of everything in about an hour or less, online! Yep! So, protect the rights to your songs by copyrighting them! In order for you to do this online, you will need to have the capability to send your songs via the Internet. A simple software program like Garageband (for Mac) or Mixcraft (for Win. 7), will let you record your voice and instrument right into your computer. If you're serious about songwriting, music software and computers are a must! You can also do the copyright via snail mail. Then, all you will need is a tape recorder, but you will still need the forms to fill out. You can obtain those online or call the Library Of Congress (202) 707-5959 or 1-877-476-0778 (toll free) (the site is **www.copyright.gov** and you can also submit everything via the online form they offer) to have them send you some. So, just to make things easier, I highly recommend the Internet, plus, it's cheaper to register online.

A copyright (license) is technically a property right with time limitations. A PA (performing arts) copyright form is for songwriters. An SR (sound recording & songwriters) copyright form is the artist's (could be you) recording of that song and VR (video recording) copyright form is for video. There are a few tricks to filing for your copyright license. As a singer/songwriter it's pretty easy! You can do it all!

Here are some of the questions on the PA (performing arts) form and SR (sound recording) form. If you can only do one, do the SR. The SR is when you have a professional recording of your songs, but it also copyrights your words and music. So, if anyone comes to use the recording you have of your songs, you will get royalties (money). Below are some of the questions asked.

Online registration is cheaper than traditional mail.

Title of work: My Music
Contents titles: 1. First song 2. Second song 3. Etc.
Completion/publication: 2010
Author: your name
   Pseudonym: a name you are also known by
   Author created: sound recording, performance, production, music, and lyrics
   Citizen of: where you're from
   Domiciled in: where you're from
Year born: your birth year
Copyright claimant: your name and address
Rights and permissions: your name, address, e-mail, phone number
Certification: your name and date

If you're recording someone else's song you need a compulsory license. This is obtainable after you get permission from the author (via their Publishers) to record their songs. To get a compulsory license you'll need to go through the Harry Fox Agency. You can be paid for being the songwriter and the artist. In film, you will need a Synch license (outlined below). Music licenses are obtained through the publisher of the song you want to license. This could also be the writer. To cover all the bases for ownership, I recommend you get a PA and SR for your songs. In order to give permission for a sync license, for example, you have to have proof of ownership. So, get your copyrights.

"1. A synchronization (synch) license: This is a license the producer of the above must obtain from the writer of the song (if the writer has assigned her © to a publisher, the producer must go through the publisher).

This license gives the producer of the above the right to synchronize the ©'d song (important: not the recording of the song, but the underlying composition—the lyrics and melody) with the moving images in the tv show, ad, or movie.

2. A master usage license: the producer of the above must negotiate a license with the person who holds the © to the recording of the above underlying composition (i.e. the version of the song found on the CD). Typically, the master usage holder is the label. If there is no label (i.e., it's self-released by the artist), then the producer of the movie, etc. negotiates directly with the artist who self-released.[23]"

For the full article go here, http://www.artistshousemusic.org/node/5368 /3318

Artists House Music provides musical information in visual and written forms and is a great website for learning just about anything pertaining to music. I really love the help with pro-tools (my music software program) I get from this website.

It's also a good place to look up the how-to on copyrights. Artists house is a great website to go to and learn just about anything pertaining to music!

What is important to know is that copyright laws are different than music or Sync Licensing. Copyrights can only be obtained through the government's Library Of Congress, while a music and/or sync license is obtained through the publisher of the song. Licensing rights between an artist and the writer are called a Mechanical License. You obtain this through the Harry Fox Agency.

---

[23]   Songs in movies, TV shows, and ads: How do the licenses work? George Howard
       (© = copyright)

Below are some license explanations from BMI. Hopefully, these will help you understand the different licensing found in the songwriting business. I'm at the point when I want to hire someone to do all this . . . I just want to write and perform!

Public Performance License

BMI, ASCAP and SESAC issue licenses on behalf of the copyright owner or his agent granting the right to perform the work in, or transmit the work to, the public.

Reproduction Right

The exclusive right of the copyright owner, granted by the Copyright Act, to authorize the reproduction of a musical work as in a record, cassette or CD.

Mechanical License (also see Compulsory Mechanical License).

Harry Fox Agency, Inc. issues licenses on behalf of the copyright owner or his agent, usually to a record company, granting the record company the right to reproduce and distribute a specific composition at an agreed upon fee per unit manufactured and sold.

Synchronization License

Music Publishers issue licenses as copyright owner or his agent, usually to a producer, granting the right to synchronize the musical composition in timed relation with audio-visual images on film or videotape.

Publisher information is available through bmi.com, ascap.com and sesac.com in their research departments.

Digital Performance Right in Sound Recordings

Sound Exchange, along with Record Companies; license the exclusive rights on behalf of copyright owners in a sound recording (which is separate from the copyright in the underlying musical works that BMI, ASCAP and SESAC represents) under U.S. Copyright Law, to authorize many digital transmissions (e.g., Internet streaming).[24]

The business end of being a musician/songwriter is not fun! I don't do well at this. Some people are naturals. I'd suggest if you're in a band to take turns or divide up the workload. If you're by yourself, do what you can. The songwriting is more important. If you play around and network yourself online maybe someone will come along who will want to do this work for you. "Work smarter, not harder," as the old saying goes.

---

[24]   http://www.bmi.com/faq/category/copyright

Highlights

The Biz—I'm too sexy for my hats!

- The Music—repertoire • rehearsals • writing • gear.
- Promotion/marketing—planning • media/publicity • distribution • merchandising • video—recording—studio research • pre-production • production • manufacturing • record labels.
- Performance—stage show • booking • touring • sound and lights.
- Legalities—licenses • contracts • insurance • taxes • trademarks.
- Business—planning • office setup • resource management • networking • publishing.
- Licenses: 3 copyright licenses for musicians, PA (publishes author), SR (sound recording) and VR (video recording) All needed to show ownership of the songs. As your own publisher you will need proof of ownership to give out permission for use of a song for Film/TV.
- I recommend you get all three copyright ownerships, PA, SR and VR, for your songs.
- Copyright license is different than a music license.

Create world peace with a song!

My vision is to see laughter, clean rain, good health, plenty of food, clean water, extra big hugs with love, and to hear everyone singing their own song, all around the world. So, don't stay silent when you could be singing your song of gratefulness and love (yep, still a hippie). It needs to be shared. Sing it out into the universe and fill up those empty spaces with your song cause, "What the world needs now is love sweet love." Create a vision board of all the things you want to see in this world and in your life (I have one!). Look at that board at least three times a day and focus on your feelings experiencing a world in peace or having that house, or that person in your life. So, write your song.

We are lucky to be songwriters because we have a way to make life better for others and ourselves. We can get up in the morning and go sit outside, while taking in the sun with a nice cup of coffee (black, thanks), and sing our songs into the air. Like a fine mist your song will fill all the spaces of the air. What you create as a song (hopefully a positive one) will change the negative blasts of airwaves created by the media. Life is really good right now, but there are some improvements to be made. There are people that have a need that we can fill. So, buy someone this book today! Anyone, at any level of songwriting, can benefit from this book but they may have no way to know about it; let alone purchase it. So this is my offer: If you buy a book for someone in need, I will give you a free t-shirt.

Promote the arts at your local schools by donating this book to them. Music was once just as important as math or science. Derived from the Greek and Roman principles, music became part of the seven liberal arts along with grammar, rhetoric, dialectic and arithmetic, geometry, and astronomy in attempt "to see the various phenomena of the world not as spate entities, but as part of the one interrelated world order." "Musica is one of the mathematical arts."[25] So, in ancient times music played an important role in society. Let's

---

[25]   Wilson, *Music Of The Middle Ages*, 4.

make sure that it stays an important part of our society by keeping the arts in school!

It is my hope that you find your happiness and joy in songwriting and pass it on to anyone and everyone! I truly believe that music saves lives by helping us become better at knowing ourselves through songs. When we write a song, we write from a place that stores a lot of hidden meanings. Sometimes these meanings are even hidden from ourselves. And so, if not tapped into, we may one day become our own worst enemy by alienating ourselves from the world. The world would be a better place with honest conversations from people who have tapped into their hidden agendas. Singer/songwriters have a mental (psychological) and physical (singing) connection with songs. You now have, with the help from this book, the ability to tap into your gift. So, give it to the world! Please join me in keeping this conversation alive by submitting to my blog, "Change The World-Write Your Song" at http://jenadouglas.wordpress.com. The best thing you could do now is to teach another person how to write their song. You know what to do!

Websites—"Help!"

Recommended websites:

Words, music and songwriting tools:

www.chordie.com,www.lyrics-p.com,www.guitarchordsmagic.com/,www.rymer.com, www.rhymezone.com, www.writeexpress.com, http://soundcloud.com/

Music camps, gigs & schools:

www.summersongs.com, www.studiomusicgroup.com/, www.reverbnation.com/,www.sonicbids.com, http://www.larkcamp.com/

Showcase your songs:

www.far-west.org/, www.folkalliance.com/, www.durangosong.com/, www.nashvillesongwriters.com/

Music publishing, licensing & business:

http://www.copyright.gov/,http://mpa.org/,www.harryfox.com/index.jsp,

Promotional and networking:

www.iacmusic.com/,www.myspace.com/,http://wordpress.org/,http://twitter.com/,www.reverbnation.com/, www.facebook.com,www.ourstage.com, www.soundclick.com, www.ezfolk.com/, http://www.songwriter.co.uk/http://www.last.fm/,www.americansongwriter.com/,http://www.nimbit.com,www.kickstarter.com/, http://interactivedigitalmusic.com/, http://www.youtube.com/

Online sales & distribution:

http://cdbaby.com/, www.tunecore.com, https://advantage.amazon. com,http://bandcamp.com/

Submitting songs:

www.sonicbids.com/,www.americansongwriter.com/,www.durangosong. com,www.taxi.com, http://www.hellomusic.com/landing.aspx

Instructional:

www.homespuntapes.com,www.enchantedlearning.com/music,www. blackbeltguitar.com,www.guitarchordsmagic.com/,www.musesmuse. com/www.nashvillesongwriters.com/,http://musicians.about.com/od/ beingamusician/a/tourpress.htm, http://www.pianoworld.com/fun/vpc/ piano_chords.htm, http://www.rhymer.com/

Online music resource information:

http://www.gearslutz.com/, www.artisthousemusic.org, http://www.songfacts.com/

Internet radio:

http://www.shoutcast.com/, http://www.live365.com/index.live, http:// submit.pandora.com/, http://www.radiosubmit.com/, http://www. indievtv.com/, http://www.bandattack.com/indieradio.htm

Books you will want to get

Excuse Me, your Life Is Waiting- the astonishing power of feelings by Lynn Grabhorn

Making a Living in your Local Music Market—Realizing your marketing potential by Dick Weissman

Music, Money And Success—The Insider's Guide to Making Money in the Music Industry by Jeffrey Brabec and Todd Brabec

Mutant Message Down Under by Morgan, Marlo

Songwriting Fundamentals—discover the true joy of songwriting by Dave Byers

Songwriter on Songwriting by Paul Zollo

The Business and Legal Guide for Songwriters and Performers- Making It in the Music Business by Lee Wilson

The Complete Singer-Songwriter by Jeffery Pepper Rodgers

The Secret by Rhonda Byrnes

The Self-Promoting Musician—Strategies for Independent Music Success by Peter Spellman

Piano—Scales and chords

Piano Scales

Here are The Major Scales:

C Major Scale: C D E F G A B	C Major Scale: C D E F G A B
D Major Scale: D E F# G A B C#	D Major Scale: D E F# G A B C#
E Major Scale: E F# G# A B C# D#	E Major Scale: E F# G# A B C# D#
F Major Scale: F G A Bb C D E	F Major Scale: F G A Bb C D E
G Major Scale: G A B C D E F#	G Major Scale: G A B C D E F#
A Major Scale: A B C# D E F# G#	A Major Scale: A B C# D E F# G#
B Major Scale: B C# D# E F# G# A#	B Major Scale: B C# D# E F# G# A#
C# Major Scale: C# D# E# F# G# A# B#	C# Major Scale: C# D# E# F# G# A# B#
Eb Major Scale: Eb F G Ab Bb C D	Eb Major Scale: Eb F G Ab Bb C D
F# Major Scale: F# G# A# B C# D# E#	F# Major Scale: F# G# A# B C# D# E#
Ab Major Scale: Ab Bb C Db Eb F G	Ab Major Scale: Ab Bb C Db Eb F G
Bb Major Scale: Bb C D Eb F G A	Bb Major Scale: Bb C D Eb F G A

Here are The *Natural* Minor Scales:

C Minor Scale: C D Eb F G Ab Bb C	B Minor Scale: B C# D E F# G A B
D Minor Scale: D E F G A Bb C D	C# Minor Scale: C# D# E F# G# A B C#
E Minor Scale: E F# G A B C D E	Eb Minor Scale: Eb F Gb Ab Bb Cb Db Eb
F Minor Scale: F G Ab Bb C Db Eb F	F# Minor Scale: F# G# A B C# D E F#
G Minor Scale: G A Bb C D Eb F G	G# Minor Scale: G# A# B C# D# E F# G#
A Minor Scale: A B C D E F G A	Bb Minor Scale: Bb C Db Eb F Gb Ab Bb

Piano Chords

Piano Chords - C and C#:

Key: C	Key: C#
C = C E G	C#= C# E# G#
Cm = C Eb G	C#m = C# E G#
C7 = C E G Bb	C#7 = C# E# G# B
CM7 = C E G B	C#M7 = C# E# G# B#
Cm7 = C Eb G Bb	C#m7 = C# E G# B
Csus = C F G	C#sus = C#F#G#
Csus7 = C F G Bb	C#sus7 = C# F# G# B
C6 = C E G A	C#6 = C# E# G# A#
C2 = C D E G	C#2 = C# D# E# G#

Piano Chords – Db and D:

Key: Db	Key: D
Db: Db F Ab	D: D F# A
Dbm: Db Fb Ab	Dm: D F A
Db7: Db F Ab Cb	D7 : D F# A C
DbM7: Db F Ab C	DM7: D F# A C#
Dbm7: Db Fb Ab Cb	Dm7: D F A C
Dbsus: Db Gb Ab	Dsus: D G A
Dbsus7: Db Gb Ab Cb	Dsus7: D G A C
Db6: Db F Ab Bb	D6: D F# A B
Db2: Db Eb F Ab	D2: D E F# A

Piano Chords - Eb and E:

Key: Eb	Key: E
Eb = Eb G Bb	E = E G# B
Ebm = Eb Gb Bb	Em = E G B
Eb7 = Eb G Bb Db	E7 = E G# B D
EbM7 = Eb G Bb D	EM7 = E G# B D#
Ebm7 = Eb Gb Bb Db	Em7 = E G B D
Ebsus = Eb Ab Bb	Esus = E A B
Ebsus7 = Eb Ab Bb Db	Esus7 = E A B D
Eb6 = Eb G Bb C	E6 = E G# B C#
Eb2 = Eb F G Bb	E2 = E F# G# B

Piano Chords - F and F#:

Key: F	Key: F#
F = F A C	F# = F# A# C#
Fm = F Ab C	F#m = F# A C#
F7 = F A C Eb	F#7 = F# A# C# E
FM7 = F A C E	F#M7 = F# A# C# E#
Fm7 = F Ab C Eb	F#m7 = F# A C# E
Fsus = F Bb C	F#sus = F# B C#
Fsus7 = F Bb C Eb	F#sus7 = F# B C# E
F6 = F A C D	F#6 = F# A# C# D#
F2 = F G A C	F#2 = F# G# A# C#

Piano Chords - G, Ab and A:

Key: G	Key: Ab	Key: A
	Ab = Ab C Eb	A = A C# E
G = G B D	Abm = Ab Cb Eb	Am = A C E
Gm = G Bb D	Ab7 = Ab C Eb Gb	A7 = A C# E G
G7 = G B D F	AbM7 = Ab C Eb G	AM7 = A C# E G#
GM7 = G B D F#	Abm7 = Ab Cb Eb Gb	Am7 = A C E G
Gm7 = G Bb D F	Absus = Ab Db Eb	Asus = A D E
Gsus = G C D	Absus7 = Ab Db Eb Gb	Asus7 = A D E G
Gsus7 = G C D F	Ab6 = Ab C Eb F	A6 = A C# E F#
G6 = G B D E	Ab2 = Ab Bb C Eb	A2 = A B C# E
G2 = G A B D		

Piano Chords - Bb and B:

Key: Bb	Key: B
Bb = Bb D F	B = B D# F#
Bbm = Bb Db F	Bm = B D F#
Bb7 = Bb D F Ab	B7 = B D# F# A
BbM7 = Bb D F A	BM7 = B D# F# A#
Bbm7 = Bb Db F Ab	Bm7 = B D F# A
Bbsus = Bb Eb F	Bsus = B E F#
Bbsus7 = Bb Eb F Ab	Bsus7 = B E F# A
Bb6 = Bb D F G	B6 = B D# F# G#
Bb2 = Bb C D F	B2 = B C# D# F#

Glossary—yep, there are big words here

Alliteration: a repetition of matching initial consonants of two or more words in a line of speech.

Allusion: indirect reference to something.

ASCAP: The American Society of Composers, Authors and Publishers a organization which licenses and collects royalties for its members.

Assonance Rhyme: see near rhyme.

BMI: Broadcast Music, Inc. a organization which licenses and collects royalties for its members.

Chorus: refrain that is repeated and includes the hook and/or title.

Compulsory license: a license (by permission) to record and distribute someone else's song. Also known as a Compulsory Mechanical License.

Consonant Rhyme: matching consonants. (ladies, loaders)

Copyright: an exclusive right to the creator of an original work.

Diatonic: using only the notes of the key and not any passing notes outside of the key.

Empathy: the ability to share the feelings of another.

Feminine Rhyme: the stress is on the second from last syllable of the words (*lucky, Truckee*).

Grand Staff: treble and bass staff connected by a brace and a line.

Hook: figurative thing designed to catch someone's attention; a chorus or repeated instrumental passage in music.

Intonation: the act of reciting words in song and being on pitch and in tune.

Key: a group of notes based on the root or tonic note making up a scale.

Ledger Lines: lines and spaces to organize musical notes.

Line: part of a verse. One sentence.

Maestro (music): a distinguished musician or conductor of classical music.

Major/Minor: modal scales in different keys. Major is brighter while minor is darker sounding.

Masculine Rhyme: the stress is on the final syllable of the words (*time*, *dime*).

Mechanical rights: the right to record and distribute someone else's song.

Metaphor: substituting the likeness of a word for another word without using "like" or "as."

Modulating: when you change from one key to another in the same song.

Mosaic Rhyme: a single multisyllabic word is made to rhyme with two or more words.

Motif: like a hook; a few notes found in the hook as memorable and decorative and then used as basis for larger musical pieces. An example of this would be the theme for Darth Vader in Star Wars.

Near rhyme: the consonant following the rhyming vowel is different.

Notes: an oval shape symbolizing a musical pitch and its duration.

Outro (or finale): last part of a piece of music.

Oxymoron: figure of speech that links together two terms, which are customarily opposites: "burning ice," etc.

Perfect Rhyme: the consonant following the rhyming vowel is the same.

Persona: a person takes on a personality other than their own.

Phrase: a unit of music varying in melody, harmony, and rhythm. In modern tunes, this also means the story of the song organized in verses and choruses.

Plagiarize: take the work or idea of someone else's as your own.

Scales: consists of 7 notes, first note being the tonic or root. Notes move in whole or half steps up or down.

Scansion: the rhythm of the words when spoken or sung.

SESAC: SESAC is not an abbreviation of anything, an organization which licenses and collects royalties for its members.

Simile: substituting the likeness of a word for another word by using "like" or "as."

Solfege: an exercise in singing using the solmization syllables.

Stanza: a group of lines in a verse.

Syllabic Rhyme: a rhyme in which the last syllable of each word sounds the same but does not necessarily contain vowels. (*lover*, *laughter*)

Symbolism: the use of symbols to represent ideas or qualities.

Synchronization license: a license needed for a song to be reproduced onto a media format such as TV, film, & video.

Syntactically: using rules for the arrangement of words and phrases in a sentence.

Treble and Bass Clef: organizes notes on staff for easy reading.

Verse: part of a phrase usually four sentences long.

Wordsmith: a skilled user of words.

Wrench Rhyme: a stressed syllable with an unstressed one. (maybe, a tree)

Bibliography

Bently, Toni. 2010. A Chart Topping Cave Dweller—interview of Diane Warren. *The Wall Street Journal*—Oct.16,2010.

Byers, Dave. *Songwriting Fundamentals:* Discover the true joy of songwriting! 2000.

Byrne, Rhonda. *The Secret.* New York: New York: Atria Books, 2006.

Douma, Michael, curator. "Poetry through the Ages." (2008). http://www.webexhibits.org/poetry (Aug.12,2011).

Grabhorn, Lynn. *Excuse Me, your Life Is Waiting-* the astonishing power of feelings. Charlottesville: Virginia: Hampton Road Publishing Company, 2000.

Hinton, Brian. *Joni Mitchell: Both Sides Now—The Biography.* London: United Kingdom: Sanctuary Publishing Limited, Sanctuary House, 1996.

Morgan, Marlo. *Mutant Message Down Under.* New York: New York: Harper Collins Publishers, 1995.

O'Connell, Charles. *The Victor Book Of The Symphony:* Revised Edition. New York: New York: Simon and Schuster, 1941.

Spellman, Peter. *The Self-Promoting Musician:* Strategies for Independent Music Success. Boston, Maine: Berklee Press, 2000.

Wilson, David Fenwick, *Music Of The Middle Ages:* Style And Structure. New York: New York: Schirmer Books, 1990.

Zollo, Paul. *Songwriters On Songwriting.* New York: New York: Da Capo Press, 1997.

Music saves lives! Save the music in schools and change a person's life by donating this book, *Change The World; Write Your Song*, to charity, a library or school of your choice. Purchase this book for someone in need and you'll get a free t-shirt! Include your check or go online and pay via PayPal (make sure you email me your receipt).

Email info to: jena@jenadouglas.com
Or mail to:
Jena Douglas C/O Walter Douglas
648 Calle Rinconada Santa Barbara, CA 93105

YOUR NAME:	_____
ADDRESS:	_____
EMAIL:	_____
THE ORGANIZATION YOU WISH TO DONATE A BOOK TO:	
NAME:	_____
ADDRESS:	_____
EMAIL:	_____